The Index Card Business Plan

For Sales Pros and Entrepreneurs

How to Use the Pillar System to
Simplify Your Strategy and Magnify Your Results

Brian Margolis

PRODUCTIVITY
GIANT

ProductivityGiant.com

ISBN: 978-0-692-07411-4

Illustrations by Marylee Margolis

You Don't Need Another Idea, You Need a Strategy!

Can your business strategy fit on an index card? Can you run your sales job from an index card? Can it really be that simple?

Yes, yes, and yes ... eventually.

Achieving simplicity isn't easy, but the rewards are extraordinary. The good news is the hard work has already been done. The blueprint for simplifying your strategy has been created.

The Index Card Business Plan lays out a proven system (the Pillar System) to develop a simple strategy – a strategy to cut through the clutter and move you toward <u>clarity</u>, <u>simplicity</u>, and most importantly ... <u>results</u>.

Who is This Book For?

Although this book has a sales pro/entrepreneur slant, the Pillar System applies to everyone from managers and executives to those trying to improve their health.

Basically, any person or organization trying to accomplish a goal will find the Pillar System to be effective at creating a simple strategy to achieve it. You can simply replace the word "business" with "project," "mission," or "organization". You can also apply the Pillar System to projects within a business or organization.

Access the Latest Bonus Materials and Training at **IndexCardBusinessPlan.com**

FOREWORD

In a million years, I never saw Brian writing a business book. When we talked almost 18 years ago about starting a business together, he was a scientist who, to my understanding, "played" with fish in oceans and rivers. I was the business guy, the sales guy. Fast forward a few years and I'd taken a job while Brian was striking deals, getting industry recognition for the company we'd started, and associating with the "big boys." He'd become the entrepreneur while I'd moved to the Midwest to stake out a career in sales.

Although we remained friends, it would be another decade before our business lives intersected again. I was making a great living selling financial products, but I wanted to go to the next level. So I approached Brian about helping me with a new strategy. It worked. Two years later, my income doubled. At the time of this writing, it has quadrupled. I can directly relate this result to what Brian and I worked on...specifically, the Pillar System described in this book.

I've always believed Brian's "special sauce" is his ability to take the increasingly complicated and cluttered mess of the average business or project and simplify it into an actionable strategy. He questions everything and accepts only assumptions that have been validated. I guess that's the scientist in him. He's a master of the counterintuitive language of success. He's taught me that less is more, that you must slow down to speed up, and that simplification is the goal in every area of my business.

When Brian began writing this book, he was fully on board, but it didn't start that way. He had little desire to write and even less desire to position himself as an expert. He readily admits that he initially developed the strategy in this book to address his own shortcomings. However, I believed this information had to get out, so I "encouraged" him for over a year until he saw the light. I believe when you understand the powerful system this book contains, you'll be glad he did.

David Ingram
Cincinnati, OH

TABLE OF CONTENTS

OVERVIEW

Achieving simplicity isn't simple. When left to human nature, complexity in any project, business, or industry will increase over time. It's challenging to reverse this, <u>but the rewards are extraordinary</u>. Consider the time and technological resources used to create the iPad – a device so simple, most kids can use it before they can spell. Think about the amount of engineering and work that was done so we can turn on our lights by simply "flicking" a switch. The evidence is all around us.

"Simplicity is the ultimate sophistication." — *Leonardo da Vinci*

The good news for you is the hard work has already been done – the blueprint for simplifying your business strategy, the Pillar System, is contained in this book.

Schedule 7/15
Send 5 NSTs
2 Hours STA
3 Workouts

Does this index card look like the weekly strategy for 40 percent year-over-year growth and losing 35 pounds? As you'll find out later in the book, it is!

The first part of the Pillar System turns the complicated and overwhelming maze of your business into a list of critical weekly activities (pillars) short enough to fit on an index card. The weekly execution of these pillars, whose completion is entirely in your control, all but guarantees you'll hit your goals in any viable business or project. The second part of the Pillar System provides a customizable strategy to turn weekly pillar execution into a habit.

In my own learning and teaching, I've found that it's easy to get so bogged down in the details that you can't see the forest for the trees. To help paint the big picture, I've laid out the chapter summaries below.

Chapter 1: "Understanding the Pillar System" explains what pillars are, the benefits of using the Pillar System, and the underlying principles that make the system so effective.

Chapter 2: "Identifying Your Pillars" gives you the tools and the step-by-step instructions for correctly identifying the right pillars for your business or project.

Chapter 3: "Case Studies" features real-world case studies of pillar identification.

Chapter 4: "Working with Your Pillars" shows you how to refine and work with your pillars to streamline, organize, and grow your business.

Chapter 5: "Executing on Your Pillars" explains the mindset and strategies needed to turn weekly pillar execution into a powerful and productive habit.

CHAPTER 1

UNDERSTANDING THE PILLAR SYSTEM

Introduction

To understand where the Pillar System fits into your business or career, you must recognize that <u>being good at something is different than being successful</u>. The skills required to run a successful business differ radically from the trade skills used within the business. For example, there are mechanics who can tell you what's wrong with your car blindfolded, but they can't necessarily run a successful auto repair shop or even remain gainfully employed. You can also see this distinction among authors. Great writers aren't compensated as well or recognized as much as writers who are good at promoting and selling a book. That's why you hear the term "best-selling author" not "best-writing author."

Many talented, hard-working, and highly skilled people have yet to reach the level of success they're capable of. A primary reason is they don't have the skills and/or strategy to run themselves or their businesses. I often find that talented professionals who are stuck don't need more ideas; they need a strategy. The Pillar System is designed for just this purpose. It uses the concept of focus management to help you develop a simple business strategy to achieve your goals.

Focus Management and the Birth of the Pillar System

An honest analysis of our work lives reveals there's more than enough time to be successful. Look around your office, or think about those with a similar job or business. The people who work the most hours aren't always the most successful, and the people who work the fewest hours aren't always at the back of the pack.

Time management has its place, but when it comes to getting results, the key is focus management, i.e., what we <u>intentionally</u> choose to focus on. Focus, not time, is our true limiting resource – specifically, our ability to get and stay focused on cognitively demanding activities (CDAs) for a given length of time. CDAs are activities that require significant mental resources such as creating, synthesis, decision making, willpower, and problem solving.

Think about your own workdays and answer the following questions:

1) What typically runs out first during the day? Is it time, or is it your ability to get and stay focused on activities that require significant mental resources?

2) What're you doing toward the end of your workday? Are you effectively creating, innovating, and prospecting (CDAs), or are you staying busy with "work-related" tasks?

To succeed with a finite amount of focus, the CDAs you choose to focus on must be <u>high-leverage</u> activities, i.e., those with a significant positive impact relative to the amount of time and energy you expend. Some CDAs have a much bigger return on investment than others. And some CDAs – such as spending 45 minutes dealing with a difficult customer – have little return on investment. Consequently, increasing your mental energy reserves or working additional hours, *without improving focus management*, won't move the needle. You'll just have more time and energy to work on low- or no-impact activities.

Think of driving. Taking the scenic route along country roads will ultimately empty your gas tank (mental energy). So will taking the highway straight through. However, taking the highway will get you much farther than the scenic route on the same tank of gas. The Pillar System makes sure you're always driving on the highway.

Let's consider this in terms of professional productivity and success. In any business or project, there are more things to do than time. So why do some of us stay busy all day without moving the needle while others make leaps and bounds, seemingly without breaking a sweat?

An objective look at both groups reveals a pretty clear distinction. People in the latter group identify high-leverage activities and focus on them at the expense of everything else. People in the former group spend most of their time "doing" and "reacting." <u>Whether it's intentional or not, they prioritize activity over results</u>.

At first glance, joining the successful group seems simple: You just identify and prioritize your high-leverage activities. However, as I worked through the process of helping myself, my partners, and my clients transition, I realized that most people can't <u>correctly</u> identify their highest leverage activities. And if they did, they lacked the ability to <u>consistently</u> execute on them week in and week out.

After considerable trial and error, a simplification of their business through the establishment of a custom set of "pillars" yielded the best results. We identified these pillars by running all their potential activities through a system of specific questions and criteria to determine the most critical, high-leverage ones on which to focus. The result was a short list of realistic weekly activities (pillars) that, when executed on consistently, all but guaranteed success in any viable business or project.

A pillar is an activity, meeting specific criteria that when executed on consistently, has a disproportionately positive impact on the health and/or growth of a business.

In a world where the true limiting resource is focus, not time, pillars proved to be the answer. When identified correctly, pillars could align what a person or organization wanted to accomplish with what they actually did on a week-to-week basis. These pillars, <u>whose completion was 100% in the person's control</u>, became a simple but powerful business plan that could fit on an index card. I added a second step of creating a Custom Accountability Program to turn weekly pillar execution into a habit and the Pillar System was born.

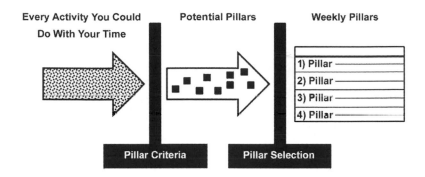

The Pillar System reduces everything you could be doing with your time down to those activities (pillars) that when executed on consistently, have the greatest impact on the health and/or growth of your business.

Cut to the Chase

In the spirit of simplicity, I tried to keep this book as short as possible. As a reader, I often wish authors would skip the extraneous theory and just "cut to the chase." However, if you don't understand the principles and concepts supporting the Pillar System, your chances of succeeding with it diminish.

I believe so profoundly in how the Pillar System has helped me and my clients that I don't want you to just "understand it." Nor do I want you to simply read this book and pass judgment. <u>I want you to use it</u>! The only way I can do this is by making sure you can answer "yes" to the following three questions*

1) Can I do it?

2) Will it work?

3) Is it worth it?

---

* These questions come from a TED Talk on self-motivation by professor Scott Geller, based on his own work and the work of psychologist Albert Bandura.

By the end of this book, you'll be able to answer all three questions in the affirmative. The simplicity of the Pillar System, as outlined in later chapters, allows you to answer "yes" to the first question ("Can I do it?"). However, your ability to answer the last two questions in the affirmative ("Will it work?" and "Is it worth it?") depends on your understanding of the benefits and principles outlined in the rest of this chapter. It's for this reason that I've decided to not just "cut to the chase."

The Benefits of Using the Pillar System

Achieving your goals is the primary benefit of correctly identifying and executing on your pillars. However, there are many benefits that contribute to your goal achievement and make the implementation of the Pillar System worthwhile.

Increased Clarity and Less Overwhelm

The Pillar System provides you with day-to-day, hour-to-hour clarity in terms of what you must do to move your business or project forward. When you lack clarity, you're easily taken off track or seduced by shiny objects. Decisions made without clarity can be detrimental to your progress.

A quick exercise to test your current level of clarity is to answer the following question. "If all my administrative tasks were done and my calendar was magically cleared for the remainder of the day, what would I work on next?" If on any given day the answer isn't crystal clear, you don't have the clarity you need. You don't have a strategy. Although you may not "feel" like working on the next most important task, you should be able to identify what it is.

Clarity facilitates progress. It also reduces the unpleasant feeling of being overwhelmed. When you're overwhelmed, you have no clarity or certainty. You can usually articulate a few things on your mind, but after that, it's just an abstract feeling that causes work paralysis and stifles decision making.

Those who use the Pillar System have considerably less overwhelm because they maintain clarity about what they should, and what they shouldn't be doing.

"With clarity and certainty there can be no overwhelm." — Susan Sly

Less Second-Guessing and Changing Directions

Well into my entrepreneurial career, I was the undisputed champion of changing directions. When I didn't see quick results, I'd second-guess my strategy, abandon it, and try something new. I often implemented new strategies based on emotion, or because of something I'd just learned about. I gave more weight to the novelty of an idea than to its actual value. A short time later, I'd second-guess the new strategy and change directions again. The repetitive cycle was mentally and emotionally exhausting.

The adoption of the Pillar System forced me to run my strategy through a very specific set of criteria before I finalized it. The result was confidence in my strategy and the reduction of second-guessing and changes in direction.

Less Time Working

A natural byproduct of identifying and executing on the right things is that you'll get further ahead with less time and effort. In fact, as a workaholic who was proud of working late and being busy, I found that my adoption of the Pillar System had early unintended consequences. When I completed my pillars before Friday, I got anxious and quickly found ways to keep busy, as years of believing "there's always stuff to do" were still ingrained in me. I'm convinced that we often keep working because, as entrepreneurs or results-based employees, we have no clear indicator that we're done. There's no squawking bird that tells our inner Fred Flintstone to slide down the dinosaur and clock out for the day. The Pillar System gives you reliable indicators to assist with this problem.

Peace of Mind

Without a doubt, the benefit about which I get the most positive feedback is the "Friday night feeling." This feeling, discussed later in the book, is the peace of mind you have at the end of your week <u>knowing</u> you made substantial progress because you completed your pillars. It's the peace of mind that, regardless of the current week's results, your business is moving in the right direction.

The Simplification of Your Role in Complex Businesses and Projects

If you're part of a larger and more complex business or project, you may find the number of moving parts to be overwhelming. The choices in terms of what you can focus on at any given moment seem endless. The Pillar System ensures that not only are you focusing on the right things, you're also delegating or outsourcing the <u>right things</u> to be done by others.

The Identification of Bad Strategies or Opportunities

A very successful mentor of mine explained something that forever changed the way I look at business opportunities. Early in his career as an engineer, he wanted to be rich. He wanted to make a million dollars a year. The problem, he told me, was that "engineers don't make a million dollars a year." So he moved to an industry with greater income potential and went on to achieve significant wealth.

Regardless of your goals, whether they're income-related or not, you must make sure the vehicle you choose can get you there. It also helps to occasionally look up and make sure you're traveling down the right road.

As I shared the Pillar System with more partners and clients, I realized a benefit I hadn't anticipated. The practice of identifying your initial pillars and then refining them over time often reveals that you've chosen the wrong vehicle (business, opportunity, or job) or gone down the wrong road (chosen strategy within the business). Specifically, if you can't find a set of pillars to help you achieve your goal, the goal probably isn't realistic. The earlier you discover this, the better.

Why the Pillar System Works

As discussed earlier, if you believe the Pillar System will work, you're more likely to implement it and stick with it long enough to see results. If you're fortunate enough to have seen a colleague or friend's results, you're off to a great start. However, in the end, you still must believe it will work for you. This section uses experiences to which you can relate, along with well-grounded success principles to explain why the Pillar System works.

The Pillar System Doubles Down on Focus

I'd be doing you a disservice if I didn't do everything possible to drive home the fact that one of the biggest controllable factors in your success will be what you choose to focus on (focus management). Focus is the open secret of success. The proof is all around you. Let's look at the Wright Brothers, the ubiquitous Rollaboard, and one casino's solution to reduce waste removal costs.

On December 17, 1903, in Kill Devil Hills, N.C., Orville and Wilbur Wright made what many consider to be the first successful flight of a piloted, self-propelled aircraft. This feat of aviation innovation was something I first learned about as a kid. However, it was only recently that I read an article and learned some interesting facts about another aviation innovation. Luggage with wheels wasn't invented until 1972, and practical luggage with wheels wasn't invented until the late 1980s! That's when Robert Plath, a pilot for Northwest Airlines, devised the two-wheel "Rollaboard." The Rollaboard is the ubiquitous piece of luggage, with wheels and a telescoping handle, most of us pull through the airport.

As groundbreaking as this invention was to air travel, it certainly wasn't as difficult to engineer as the first airplane. So why did it take almost 90 years after the first flight to successfully put wheels on luggage? Because, until then, nobody focused on it for any significant period of time! Certainly, had President John F. Kennedy focused on the luggage problem in the early 60's instead of trying to land on the moon, the issue would have been resolved much quicker. Robert Plath's success wasn't a result of his engineering talents, but instead a result of focusing on the right thing.

I have some personal experience with this. Several years ago, I helped a large casino client significantly reduce their waste removal costs. One of the initiatives I implemented was having the heavy solid food waste removed by a farmer who could feed it to his pigs. This simple change, which took a little research and a few phone calls, literally cut this portion of the casino's bill in half. So why didn't the large and capable staff of the casino's finance and facilities departments solve the problem without me? Because it wasn't something on which they were focused!

Ultimately, your progress will depend on what you intentionally choose to focus on week in and week out. And the Pillar System ensures you're consistently focused on the right things.

"Where focus goes, energy flows." — *Tony Robbins*

The Pillar System Works with Human Nature, Not Against It

You've no doubt seen the motivational seminars that preach about how you were "built for success" or "destined to succeed." However, just a basic understanding of human biology shows what a load of crap that is. The reason success is celebrated, and rightfully so, is it requires us to overcome our natural human tendencies. The Pillar System is designed to work with your brain as it is, not as you want it to be.

Your brain is designed for survival. Without conscious intervention, its default setting is to avoid change, discomfort, and pain. And because your brain works on autopilot most of your life, working outside this comfort zone for extended periods of time is difficult. I've read all sorts of stats about how much of our day is habitual and I don't know where the truth lies. However, if you want to know how automated you are, just move the trash can in your kitchen. For days, if not weeks, you'll literally walk toward a trash can that isn't there.

Another problem in the battle of "the brain vs the workday" is that your ability to focus on the higher level, cognitively demanding activities discussed earlier is finite. These activities use parts of your brain, like the prefrontal cortex, that burn through a limited energy supply very quickly. The result is that you have only so many hours in a day to effectively work on cognitively demanding activities.

The Pillar System overcomes these obstacles in two ways. First, it forces you to use your limited mental resources on activities that have the highest leverage and impact (pillars). Second, the Pillar System helps you do this consistently enough so that pillar execution is pushed into the automated part of your brain that uses energy much more efficiently (i.e., habit formation). By doing this, you're working with your brain's strengths to get an unfair advantage. The strategy for forming this habit is outlined in chapter 5.

The Pillar System Facilitates Momentum

Pillars facilitate momentum because they're measured weekly and their execution is <u>completely within your control</u>. A week is a real and excuseless unit of measurement that provides immediate feedback. This quick, positive feedback increases the chance you'll continue taking action, resulting in another week of pillar execution. Eventually, your belief grows along with your progress, and taking action becomes more desirable. This starts a positive feedback loop that continues to build upon itself. The upward spiral has begun.

The Pillar System Emphasizes Productivity Over Activity

"Being busy is a form of laziness — lazy thinking and indiscriminate action."
— *Tim Ferris*

Earlier I explained that when we feel overwhelmed or stuck, it's often due to a lack of clarity. We aren't confident about the next step and we change directions constantly based on new ideas, shiny objects, and outside requests. We stay very busy, but at the end of the day, we're mentally exhausted and often depressed about our lack of progress.

Identifying and refining your pillars emphasizes slowing down to speed up. It values taking the time to clarify where your efforts are best placed instead of just "doing more." Although merit-based jobs and the free market reward you for productivity and not activity, only a small percentage of us truly incorporate this knowledge into our work lives. Most of us have no problem justifying the hour we spend every morning responding to emails. But what about spending 15 minutes strategically thinking about our priorities for the day? Making a hundred calls a week sounds noble, but what about spending a few hours identifying the best prospects and crafting an effective message before picking up the phone? Pillars are the ultimate tool for the strategy David Rock, author of *Your Brain at Work,* has termed "prioritize prioritizing."

The creation of pillars gives us the best answers to questions like "On what should I spend my time?" and "What should I *not* do?" Pillars force us to work <u>on</u> our business instead of just <u>in</u> our business — a concept made famous in Michael Gerber's seminal books, *The E-Myth* and *The E-Myth Revisited.*

Over time, your pillars become such a priority that all the unimportant emails, requests, shiny objects, and inner dialogues vying for your attention stand no chance. You become a master of cutting bait, saying no, and unsubscribing to the email list of the world.

Many people wear busyness like a badge of honor. Those who use pillars also wear a badge — a badge that honors everything to which they say no or that they don't act upon. More importantly, their badge honors progress. Work for the sake of work and change for the sake of change don't mean anything without progress ... and progress is the most motivating thing you can experience.

The Pillar System Forces You to Use the 80/20 Principle

Most professionals superficially agree with the 80/20 principle, which states that 20% of your efforts are responsible for 80% of your results. However, I meet few people who <u>actually apply</u> this principle to their businesses or lives on a consistent basis.

An examination of almost any business or project reveals the 80/20 principle is true; in fact, it's often closer to 95/10 or 99/5. However, our industrial age conditioning has made it difficult to overcome the dogma of a linear relationship between effort and results. The reality is that small hinges swing big doors, and a concentrated and consistent effort to apply the 80/20 principle to your decision making will allow for exponential instead of linear growth. The establishment and execution of your weekly pillars ensure you're applying the 80/20 principle.

"Take a great mental leap: Disassociate effort from reward." — *Richard Koch*

The Pillar System Allows You to Measure Progress Accurately

In many businesses and projects, a lag time exists between actions and results. This makes it difficult to assess progress on a weekly basis. The result is that we tend to judge our progress based on emotions rather than on reality. A big sale you've been working on is finalized, so you celebrate a great week and paint the future with optimism. Nobody calls for a while and you think your efforts have been fruitless.

Neither scenario reflects reality, but they're all you have to go on when you only focus on lag indicators, i.e., metrics that are compounding results of prior actions. These metrics – such as sales, inquiries, sign-ups – are often an inaccurate reflection of your current week's productivity.

To accurately measure productivity and track progress, you must also look at lead indicators. For our purposes, lead indicators are the actions – such as phone calls made, time spent improving your message - that drive output metrics. When pillars are established correctly, they become the primary lead indicators of your business. The very concept of pillars is that if you complete them each week, you're progressing.

The Pillar System Helps You Run an Intentional Business

Humans are creatures of habit. An honest look at ourselves reveals that we do most things habitually or in reaction to outside stimuli. Running an intentional business is the opposite of being reactive, doing things habitually or winging it. It prioritizes <u>strategy</u> and <u>results</u> over activity.

You can choose to be reactive (check your email, answer the phone, entertain ideas that pop into your head) at <u>certain times</u> or <u>all the time</u>. Most people choose the latter. Those who operate within the Pillar System appropriate specific times for being reactive. Running an intentional business is a mindset in which you do things deliberately, for a pre-determined reason ... or you don't do them.

Professionals who run intentional businesses benefit from a simplicity and clarity that few professionals experience. It's the planning, precision, and clarity of a special forces mission versus unloading all your bullets and grenades from behind a wall. The latter scenario is filled with non-stop activity, and certainly gives you the sense of having fought hard, but accomplishing the mission is far from guaranteed. In our own businesses, we're often so busy that we trick ourselves into believing we're getting somewhere ... and that's a dangerous place to be.

Executing on your pillars is the ultimate foundation for an intentional business. Your weekly and daily focus is based on a well-thought-out strategy that's in line with what you want to accomplish. You don't have to question every decision; the decisions are made in advance.

Running an intentional business is analogous to creating a playlist on your mp3 player. It takes time and preparation to select and download the songs, but the car ride is guaranteed to be filled with the right music. The alternative is to jump in the car and play with the radio for three hours, hoping to occasionally find a good song. The latter requires little mental energy and keeps you much busier, but produces inferior results.

"... the downfall for many individuals is that they just take on more business, more obligations, and more situations. They get overwhelmed, and they procrastinate." — Jeffery Combs

The Pillar System Aligns Your Goals with What You Actually Do

As an outside observer for many professionals, I commonly see a disconnect between what professionals claim they want to accomplish and what they actually do on a daily basis. The amazing part isn't the disconnect, but the fact that the person doesn't see it!

I experienced the consequences of this type of disconnect in one of my early ventures. It "felt" like we were doing great. However, only a few years later we'd be selling off in a fire sale what was left of the business. Top people and organizations in the field were using our product and our brand was receiving recognition outside of our direct influence. This was flattering, but the clear goal was to make a large enough profit so that I could continue growing the business full time. In hindsight, we focused too much of our activity on branding and accomplishments that made us "look good" and not enough on creating distribution channels that could bring in enough sales to cover the high inventory costs.

Aligning your activities with your goals seems to be an elementary skill, but it isn't. Fortunately, you're about to learn how the identification, execution, and refining of your pillars will put them in alignment.

Chapter 1: Critical Points

- Being good at something is different than being success-ful. It requires a different set of skills and an effective strategy. This is the reason so many hard-working, talent-ed people don't realize a greater level of success.

- Success requires a strategy based on focus management, not time management. This is because focus, not time, is your true limiting resource. What you choose to focus on determines your success.

- The Pillar System is a simple strategy based on focus management. It reduces everything you could be doing with your time down to those activities (pillars) that, when executed on consistently, have the biggest impact on the health and/or growth of your business.

- In addition to enabling you to hit your goals, using the Pillar System offers such benefits as:
  - Increased clarity and less overwhelm
  - Less second guessing and changing directions
  - Less time spent working
  - Peace of mind
  - The simplification of your role in complex businesses and projects
  - The identification of bad strategies or opportunities

- The Pillar System is effective because it ensures that your week-to-week strategy takes advantage of well-established success principles.

CHAPTER 2

IDENTIFYING YOUR PILLARS

Establishing Directional and Short-Term Goals

It's no accident that with respect to pillar identification, the words "correct" and "correctly" appear throughout this book. Grasping what a pillar is – and what it isn't – takes time, practice, trial, and error.

There's nuance in Pillar identification. Pillars aren't just glorified to-do lists, and if they're identified incorrectly, their benefits become watered down or non-existent.

You can't simply "copy" someone else's pillars. A pillar for one person isn't necessarily a pillar for another. It's not about finding "the" key, but about finding "your" key. The pillars you identify will be unique to your circumstances and goals. Consequently, the correct identification of your pillars requires you to establish clear goals and articulate them in a manner that works well with the Pillar System.

Directional Goals

If you're like many people, at the beginning of each year you set ambitious long-term goals. However, soon you find yourself ignoring them, shelving them, or justifying their demise. If you relate to this frustrating pattern, you can take solace in the knowledge that long-term goals aren't as crucial to your success as many would have you believe.

Despite what many people preach about the importance of long-term goals, the science just doesn't support their effectiveness. In fact, many experts argue that long-term goals are detrimental to your success! These experts recommend short-term incremental goals and a heavy focus on a consistent process or system (e.g., the Pillar System). While I agree with these assertions and espouse a system-focus in this book, I don't subscribe to the idea of completely abandoning long-term goals. I see value in a specific type of long-term goal – the directional goal.

Directional goals are realistic long-term goals that consider trajectory and direction. They act as your North Star, keeping you moving in the right direction, but they're not your ongoing measuring stick. Directional goals may or may not have hard deadlines. They can be numeric, such as dollars or number of subscribers, or non-numeric, such as finishing the writing of a book.

In a world full of shiny objects and "good" ideas, a person or business without clear and well-thought-out directional goals can quickly be blown off course by the changing winds. When you're clear on what you want for the long term, day-to-day disruptions disguised as opportunities don't sway you. You should always be asking: "Is what I'm about to do, or what I'm about to commit resources to, moving me toward or away from my directional goals?"

In addition to helping you make decisions, a continued focus on your directional goal often reveals a better way to hit that goal. Your current knowledge and beliefs will form the basis of – and will limit – the pillars you establish. However, your knowledge and beliefs may change. Don't forget, the goal is the goal! If you find a strategy or technique to speed up the realization of your goal, will you create pillars to implement it? Of course you will.

You'd be foolish to not periodically explore better ways of achieving your goals. If you don't, you'll soon be a victim of your own dogma. You'll do things a certain way for reasons that are past their expiration date.

"Those critical choices you made then, they were based on what you knew about the world as it was. But now, you know more and the world is different." — *Seth Godin*

You can intentionally look for better ways to achieve your directional goals through learning, studying others, and mastermind sessions. You can also use your sub-conscious brain, specifically your Reticular Activating System (RAS), to find better ways. However, if you don't have a clearly defined directional goal, your RAS can't help.

In recent years, much has been written about the RAS. For the sake of brevity, here are the basics. Every second of every day, the outside world bombards your brain with sounds, sights, tactile stimuli, and so on. You don't notice most of it because your RAS filters it out. So, what do you notice? You notice whatever you've voluntarily or involuntarily *told* your brain to notice.

Because of your RAS, you can sit in a restaurant with 15 conversations swirling around you, yet hear only the people at your table. It's also the reason why, when you buy a metallic blue car, you suddenly see the same car everywhere. These metallic blue cars were always there, but your RAS was filtering them out.

The power of the RAS is that you can intentionally "tell" your brain what to look for. This means if you have clear directional goals, you'll start noticing previously hidden opportunities for hitting them. This is a phenomenon described by the ubiquitous saying "you can't find what you're not looking for."

When you do find quicker strategies to hit your directional goal, don't commit to implementing them immediately. If a strategy or idea is worthwhile, it'll still be that way a week from now or a month from now. It's amazing how many great ideas don't seem so great a month later. With that in mind, record your ideas and budget time to explore them, but don't make changes until you're convinced the ideas are worthy of implementation.

Take the Directional Goal Process to the End

To take advantage of the power of your RAS, you must think your directional goals through to the end. For example, a real estate professional might have a directional goal of $15 million in sales. In addition to the commissions, they want the company and peer recognition of being a "gold medal" agent that comes with this number. In this case, $15 million in sales is the directional goal. However, if the real estate agent is driven only by the commissions, the directional goal is the income, not the $15 million in sales.

I make this distinction for a reason. Many ways exist to make money in real estate, including finding tenants for landlords, flipping houses, and subdividing plots of land to sell. At the time the agent set their goal, selling houses may have been the best opportunity to hit that income goal. However, if the agent is clear that the <u>income</u> is their directional goal, their RAS can go to work behind the scenes, scanning for other opportunities. If they leave their directional goal at $15 million in sales, the agent may miss an opportunity to partner on a lucrative investment. They may also miss opportunities outside of real estate.

Use Your Own Words

One of my directional goals is "Obtaining the freedom and means to do something awesome." The fact that this directional goal isn't easy to explain to other people used to bother me – until I realized I don't have to explain it. I'd like to do a lot of things in my lifetime, such as solve a mystery, help preserve critical tracts of land, and mentor young problem solvers (i.e., scientists and entrepreneurs). It's a list of things so long, I couldn't possibly do everything on it. The fun for me will be getting to the point financially where I can start deciding what to do first … and that's exactly what this statement means to me.

Write your directional goals in your own language so that they resonate with you. In my case, money is the tool, but for others, money is the end game. There's no judgment in this exercise, so be true to yourself. If being ranked number one in your company is more motivating than a certain dollar amount, make that one of your directional goals. Why wouldn't you want your goals to resonate? You're going to be working on them almost every day.

Short-Term Goals

Short-term goals are important for keeping yourself on track, letting you know if something needs fixing, and strengthening your motivation and resolve to succeed. Short-term goals – whether they're daily, weekly, monthly, or quarterly – direct your RAS to see opportunities that may have been missed. Short-term goals may also drive you to take the extra step, such as not leaving a meeting without asking for the business.

In some cases, you can use a short-term goal like a pace car for a directional goal. For example, if your directional goal is $150,000 in yearly sales, you can establish a weekly goal of $3,000 in sales. Even if your current weekly results are lower, say $1,200 in sales, you can choose to start at the place where you desire to be in the future. Some would argue that this sets you up for disappointment. However, I've found that the combination of pillars as your weekly measure of progress, and short-term goals as your pacer, is extremely effective. This combination allows you to measure progress realistically while still using the power of your RAS to accelerate goal attainment.

For some situations, it's more appropriate to use short-term goals as milestones instead of pacers. For example, as I'm writing this, I have a quarterly goal to finish the first draft of this manuscript along with an income goal. At the end of the quarter, I'll likely create another quarterly income goal along with a book-related goal, such as completing the first round of edits. At the same time, I'll review and refine my pillars to make sure they align with accomplishing these new goals.

The Activity Categories

The correct identification of pillars requires an understanding that all your work-related activities fall into one of three categories: insignificant activities, urgent and significant activities (US), and proactive and significant activities (PRO)*. Your awareness of these three categories is <u>crucial</u> to pillar identification and execution.

---

* These categories are a simplified adaptation of Dr. Stephen Covey's time management quadrants as outlined in his seminal book, *The 7 Habits of Highly Effective People* (New York: Free Press, 1989).

Insignificant Activities

Activities in the insignificant category range from checking on your fantasy football team to tasks that eventually require completion ... just not right now. Insignificant activities are the time- and energy-sucking vampires of your day. These activities often "feel" like they must be done right away, but they aren't important for production in any significant way. Insignificant activities are often the "loudest" in terms of seeking your attention. Think of the ding of a new text message, the bold headline of an unopened email, or a growing to-do list. However, an objective look shows that <u>no relationship exists</u> between how loud these activities call out for your attention and their importance to your business.

Insignificant activities are often <u>reactive</u> activities, such as answering phone calls, constantly checking email, and acting on ideas or thoughts that pop into your head. A "quick" look at an email or website can send you down the rabbit hole for long periods of time. Granted, it feels good to react to these stimuli or to cross things off a list, but at the end of the day, the needle of progress hasn't moved. You can spend all day being busy in this category, doing "work-related" tasks. Whether it's habitual or a way to avoid significant activities you don't like doing, this is a dangerous category in which to spend too much time.

Urgent and Significant Activities (US)

Urgent and significant, or US, activities directly affect your income and/or productivity in a significant way. They must be done *at* or *by* a certain date or time, and if they aren't, <u>there's an immediate consequence</u>. Examples include a scheduled meeting with a client or getting a piece of information to a prospect so that a sale can be completed. The activities in this category usually aren't a problem because the immediate consequence of not completing them forces us to act. Outside of keeping a calendar and a checklist, we don't need to put much thought into this category because we're hard-wired for it. It's the reason we stayed up until three in the morning the day before a school project was due even though we had six weeks to complete it.

Hint: You can remember the category by its acronym, US … since it's the category we're naturally good at.

Proactive and Significant Activities (PRO)

Proactive and significant, or PRO, activities affect your productivity and results in a significant way, but <u>don't have immediate consequences</u> if they aren't completed. These activities tend to work on the compound effect, meaning they have a big impact over time and drive the long-term health and growth of your business. Examples include making prospecting calls, sharpening your skills, generating new leads, creating good content, and strategic thinking or planning. To complete these activities, we must be <u>proactive</u>; otherwise, they won't get done.

The PRO category separates the pros from the amateurs. Because there are no immediate consequences for procrastinating on PRO activities, we tend to push them aside when our day becomes reactive. In other circumstances, we work on insignificant activities to avoid PRO activities we don't feel like doing. <u>The key to working effectively in this crucial category is the identification and execution of pillars</u>.

Think about your own business and where you fall short. Whatever the problem is, it likely falls into this category even if you don't realize it. For example, clients often tell me their problem is they're unorganized. However, a lack of organization in and of itself isn't a problem. There's only a problem if the lack of organization is preventing you from doing something significant to your production. Some of the most successful people in the world are considered by those around them to be unorganized or aloof, but it doesn't stop them from consistently executing on the high-leverage, money-making activities. Alternatively, some of the least successful people have a clean desk and a color-coded filing system.

Hint: You can remember the PRO category because these activities require you to be <u>pro</u>active. This category contains the activities on which we tend to <u>pro</u>crastinate … and most importantly, it's where the <u>pros</u> excel.

The Three Activity Categories: Your Health

To reinforce your understanding of the three activity categories, I lay them out below using the example of your health.

<u>Insignificant</u>: These activities range from stocking bandages and first aid supplies to checking the expiration dates in your medicine cabinet. They must be done, but not right this second. However, just as in your business, if you wait too long to complete insignificant tasks, they can quickly become urgent and significant. You never restocked your Caladryl lotion and now you've got poison ivy!

<u>Urgent/Significant (US)</u>: If you twist your ankle and it swells up, you ice it. If you slice open your hand, you go to the ER for stitches. If you require dialysis once a week, you probably aren't going to skip it. Just like in your business, you take care of the tasks that have immediate consequences if you don't address them.

<u>Proactive/Significant (PRO)</u>: The current state of your health and fitness (i.e., blood sugar, weight, energy, chronic issues, etc.) is primarily a result of the compound effect of your diet, sleep, stress levels, routine screenings, and exercise rituals. Of course, outside factors such as genetics and the environment are at play, just as there are external factors in business. However, for most of us, the primary drivers such as diet and exercise are classic PRO activities. You'll experience no immediate consequence if you eat a donut, nor will you notice a different person in the mirror tonight if you work out today. However, just as in business, PRO activities play a major role in determining overall health.

The Six Characteristics of a Pillar

There are six characteristics that all pillars must have. At first glance, it might seem like a lot of nuance and hair-splitting. However, as you incorporate the Pillar System into your business, you'll realize that these nuances are what make the system so effective.

The six characteristics are a built-in self-correction mechanism that you should use when identifying, reviewing, and refining your pillars. Although exceptions may exist that I've yet to come across, I can say the following with confidence:

Show me a pillar that's been executed on consistently that doesn't significantly improve your business, and I guarantee it doesn't meet at least one of the six criteria.

The Six Characteristics of a Pillar
1) A Pillar is an Activity in the Proactive/Significant Category (PRO)
2) A Pillar is a High-Leverage Activity
3) A Pillar is Something You Already Know How to Do Effectively
4) A Pillar Can Be Measured on a Weekly Basis
5) A Pillar is an Action or Predictable Result
6) A Pillar isn't a Habit

1) A Pillar is an Activity in the Proactive/Significant Category (PRO)

Pillars focus your limited mental energy on activities that are proactive and significant (PROs). Quite simply, this is because professionals rarely have trouble completing the urgent and significant (US) activities that are scheduled, that have immediate consequences, or that have a deadline.

2) A Pillar is a High-Leverage Activity

Pillars are PRO activities that, when executed on consistently, have the largest impact on your business. In fact, pillars should have a <u>dispropor- tionate</u> impact on your business in comparison to other PRO activities. For example, a sales pro may have a high closing ratio on a big-ticket item, but see only a handful of qualified prospects each week. Sure, they could improve their results by working on skills to increase their closing ratio, but a pillar that focuses on seeing more qualified prospects will have a disproportionately larger effect on business than spending time and energy getting the closing ratio from 40% to 43%.

Conversely, if a sales pro is seeing plenty of qualified prospects but isn't generating enough sales, they'd establish a different pillar to increase their closing ratio. For example, this pillar might be to dedicate a certain number of hours each week to make their presentation more effective. This type of sharpening-the-ax pillar is a classic example of something with a large, positive long-term impact that's easily pushed aside because the consequences of procrastinating aren't immediate.

When you identify your pillars, avoid the very common mistake of choosing an activity that will "improve" your business but not one that will improve it in a significant way using a realistic amount of effort. High-leverage activities are those with a high return on the energy or resources you spend on them.

Another mistake is to assume that the more time or energy needed to execute on something, the more impactful the pillar is. I'll address this concept again later, but you should understand that a pillar requiring 20 minutes to complete can have a bigger impact than a pillar requiring five hours to complete.

3) A Pillar is Something You Know How to Do Effectively

For many of us, the bottleneck in our business is an activity we already know how to do effectively, but don't do enough of for various psychological and logistical reasons. In this case, establishing a pillar to do the activity more, or more consistently, is appropriate.

When you find that a bottleneck in your business is an activity you <u>don't</u> know how to do effectively, simply doing "more" of it won't get you very far. Therefore, it doesn't qualify as a pillar. Maybe lead generation is a bottleneck in your business, but you don't know how to do it effectively. In these scenarios, we implement a "learning pillar" because you do know how to learn! The learning pillar is a common one and is covered in its own section below.

Note: "Effectively" doesn't mean "mastery." It means you're proficient enough that the activity qualifies as "high leverage," as described above.

4) A Pillar Can Be Measured on a Weekly Basis

My experience clearly suggests that weekly pillars are the most effective. When you measure progress in larger units, such as monthly, the likelihood of procrastination and creative justification for not completing tasks increases. This is something we've all experienced and it will more likely be in play if you try to create monthly pillars.

When you measure pillars daily (e.g., schedule two future phone consultations per day), there comes a point in some days when realize you may not complete it. This could be the result of a morning appointment that went long or a day of below average response. To continue this example, let's say it's three in the afternoon and you have no phone consultations scheduled with one hour to go in your workday. This scenario causes many people to "throw in the towel" because two phone consultations aren't likely. So you spend the next hour doing busy work instead of productive work. When you have weekly pillars (scheduling 10 future phone consultations per week), you still have an incentive to schedule another consultation that you can "bank" for the weekly total. At the other end of the spectrum, let's say you hit your two scheduled consultations by noon and your afternoon appointment cancels at the last minute. You can now spend time "banking" more consultations to free up time later in the week if the meeting needs to be rescheduled.

The other advantage of measuring pillars on a weekly basis is that it's in line with the reality that every day of the week isn't conducive to working on pillars (e.g., travel days, pack-and-ship days). This isn't to say you shouldn't take advantage of daily rituals and habits. It simply says to measure the results in terms of a week. In fact, daily rituals, habit creation, and time blocking are strategies discussed in chapter 5. If a pillar lends itself to being a daily activity, you can simply measure it as a realistic minimum (e.g., review an important file at least four days a week).

For most people, I recommend starting weeks on Saturdays instead of Mondays. This way, you can choose to get a jump start on your pillars over the weekend instead of finding yourself forced to use the weekend to complete the previous week's pillars. The latter situation is neither fun nor inspiring, and it will feel like a punishment.

5) A Pillar is an Action or Predictable Result

Hitting your pillars each week must be completely within your control. Consequently, a pillar must be an action or a predictable result. This can get a little confusing, so let me define each.

Action: Something you control 100%. Assuming you have enough leads, making 20 prospecting calls a week is something you control. Spending two hours a week creating marketing materials is something you control. But be careful. Just because something is an action doesn't mean it's high leverage (and therefore not a pillar). If making 20 calls doesn't move your business forward in a significant way, it isn't a pillar.

Result: Making three sales a week isn't an action; it's a result that isn't 100% in your control. Unpredictable results aren't pillars, they're goals.

Predictable Result: If you have an existing client base, you may want to schedule five future client meetings a week. Getting five clients to agree to a future meeting during the current week isn't 100% in your control. However, if you know, based on experience that you can schedule five future meetings so long as you contact enough clients, it's a <u>predictable</u> result.

If something isn't a predictable result, work backward until you can control the outcome. If you aren't sure you can schedule five future client meetings, measure the number of connections, or clients with whom you communicate about a future meeting. If this isn't predictable, measure the number of clients to whom you reach out, which is 100% in your control.

6) A Pillar isn't a Habit

Your pillars are activities that require most of your focus. If something is already a habit in your business or life, by definition, you don't need to proactively focus on it.

For example, exercise is a PRO activity that makes for a great pillar. If you don't work out today, you won't gain three pounds. However, over a long period of time, working out or not working out has a huge impact on your health and appearance. Everybody knows a person who's addicted to running (maybe it's you?). They must get in their runs or they don't feel right. Unlike most of us, who love good excuses to skip workouts, the runners I'm describing would be late to a family dinner so they can get in a run. In the case of this person, running is already habitual and therefore doesn't require much mental focus. Consequently, it wouldn't be one of their pillars.

5 Steps to Identify Your First Set of Pillars

> Download Your Pillar Identification
> Worksheet and Other Bonuses at
> **IndexCardBusinessPlan.com**

Note: This would be a good time to revisit the definition of a pillar from earlier in the book. A Pillar is an activity, <u>meeting specific criteria</u> that when executed on consistently, has a <u>disproportionately</u> positive impact on the health and/or growth of your business. At this point, the "specific criteria" and "disproportionately" parts should make more sense ... and both will be important themes of this section.

Five Steps to Identify Your First Set of Pillars

1) Create a List of Potential Pillars

2) Add Activity Levels

3) Adjust or Eliminate Those That Don't Meet All Six Criteria

4) Rank Your Potential Pillars by Impact

5) Select Your Pillars

Step One: Create a List of Potential Pillars

The best way to start identifying potential pillars is to ask the question posed below, then <u>take the time</u> to come up with the right answer.

"What's one thing I already know how to do effectively that, if I executed on more consistently or did more of, would have the biggest impact on my business ... even if nothing else changed?"

When you answer this question, think about bottlenecks. For example, if you have a great message, product, and closing ratio, but haven't scheduled enough quality appointments, you have a bottleneck. You can keep getting better in the other areas, but you'll always be limited by not having set enough appointments.

The question above requires a very specific answer, so be careful not to respond with a generality. For example, you might initially answer the question with "I need more referrals." However, to identify potential pillars, you must thoughtfully answer the question as it's stated. You're looking for activities that you already know how to do and that can move the needle. In the case of referrals, it could be consistently asking current clients and your existing network for referrals. Thus, your first potential pillar may be to ask for two referrals a week.

Ask and answer the question at least five times to begin developing your list of potential pillars. Then move on to expand your list with the potential learning and strategic pillars below.

Learning Pillars

In many cases, an activity that would positively affect your business is something you can't do effectively. Because one characteristic of a pillar is it's "something you already know how to do effectively," this activity doesn't qualify as a pillar. Continuing with the earlier example, if you don't know how to effectively ask for referrals, simply asking for two referrals a week can't be a pillar. Although you can't effectively ask for a referral, <u>you do know how to learn</u>, and this is where the learning pillar comes in.

The reality is that most skills bottlenecking your business are learnable. The problem is they aren't learnable by simply attending one seminar or reading one article. But what if you consistently dedicate time each week to learning the skill? There's no shortage of articles, training, and books on effectively orchestrating referrals. If you dedicated two hours a week to learning and practicing that would be 25-plus hours of concentrated learning in just three months! If a lack of referrals is holding back your business, what could be a better use of your time?

The problem is that our industrial age mentality has warped our definition of work. If your boss saw you pounding away at emails, they'd assume you were working. If they saw you reading a book or watching an online video, they'd think you were on your lunch break. But what's more valuable?

Honestly, when is the last time you dedicated consistent time and effort to learning a new skill? There's no shortage of information out there on just about everything you need.

Learning for learning's sake is great. However, intentional learning is what moves the needle. The key to the learning pillar is selecting the right skill around which to create a pillar. You can learn many things to help your business, but you want to choose skills that will have the biggest impact relative to the time spent improving them. <u>Selecting the right skill or skills to learn is the most important part of improving your skills</u>.

This brings us to the next question to identify potential pillars. It's essentially a different version of the original question:

"What's one skill that, if I significantly improved on, would have the biggest impact on my business ... even if nothing else changed?"

When answering this question, you must consider the ratio between the time and the resources required to become proficient, and the impact the new skill will have. If it's the type of skill that requires long periods of dedicated time (e.g., coding software), you should consider outsourcing or delegating it.

Learning pillars don't have to result in mastery. Often, simple proficiency at something will have a big impact on your business. For many of my clients and partners, improving their copywriting skills could positively impact their business. The ability to write an effective email or marketing piece that gets a good response can have a large impact. Yet most of my clients and partners never learned the most basic direct response copywriting skills. If they spent one hour a week studying this, it would drastically improve their results.

The Strategic Pillar

You've probably read some version of the quote, "Give me an hour to chop down a tree and I'll spend the first 45 minutes sharpening the ax." The version and source of the quote vary, but the message is the same. The right tools, strategy, and preparation allow you to accomplish more with less time and effort. Dan Sullivan, founder of Strategic Coach, teaches that strategy doesn't take time, it makes time. This makes sense on a logical level, but the reality is that many of us operate in a "ready, fire, aim" mode. Our natural setting is to go, go, go … do, do, do. Rarely do we slow down long enough to plan and review our activities strategically. We put more weight on sending an email to 100 prospects than on sending a few custom emails to carefully researched prospects. We don't place enough emphasis on a <u>regular schedule</u> of thinking, strategizing, organizing, and planning.

Think back to some of your bigger successes. They may have come from one encounter, one email, or one phone call out of countless attempts to move the needle. The key is to make these types of successes intentional by being strategic instead of just active. When I think about being active, I picture the old armies that lined up and charged into a hail of artillery fire on command. When I think of "strategic," I think about investing time and thought into carefully placing snipers and positioning soldiers to confuse and trap the opposing army. It takes more time up front, but you increase your chances of success with fewer soldiers.

To identify potential strategic pillars, answer this question:

"What's something I could organize, plan, or create prior to taking action that would make the action much more effective?"

If you're in sales, you might establish a pillar to create a "hit list" that considers data, time, and circumstance to determine the best prospects to contact during the current week. This way, once you get into action, you've already done the thinking and you don't have to decide whom to call or email next. Creating the hit list may take only

30 minutes, but the compound effect of consistently calling on better prospects each week instead of winging it will have a big effect on your business.

"You multiply your time by giving yourself the emotional permission to spend time on things today that will give you more time tomorrow." — Rory Vaden

---

Pillar Criteria

When identifying potential pillars, you should consider whether assigning criteria to them will increase their effectiveness. For example, instead of a pillar to connect with 10 potential customers a week, you might specify the potential customer's minimum company size. If you're considering a pillar of creating three pieces of content a week, you can specify that at least one of the three pieces must be a video.

STEP 2: Add Activity Levels

Some pillars are pass or fail. You either complete the activity or you don't (e.g., create a hit list). Other pillars must be assigned activity levels, such as time spent on the activity or the number of repetitions that must be completed (e.g., send 15 prospecting emails).

When initially identifying pillars, don't get too caught up in assigning activity levels. For example, should you set two or four appointments per week? Should you create three or five pieces of content? Should you spend 60 or 90 minutes a week working on your messaging? The reality is, you don't always have a good feel for what'll move the needle and how much time some pillars will take.

Many people overestimate what they can accomplish in a week. Thus, it's best to start at the low end. If you hit your pillars consistently, you can gradually increase your activity levels. And for the sake of developing the pillar execution habit, it's better to hit a smaller activity level (three for three) than to miss a larger one (five for six), even if the raw number is higher in the latter situation. Activity levels are minimums and you aren't penalized for exceeding them.

STEP 3: Adjust or Eliminate Those Pillars That Don't Meet All Six Criteria

Once you have a list of potential pillars with activity levels, double check they meet all six criteria. If they don't, throw them out or adjust them to meet the criteria. This is a good time to remind you that nuance is paramount. Take the time to run through the criteria and match them up to potential pillars.

The Six Characteristics of a Pillar

1) A Pillar is an Activity in the Proactive/Significant Category (PRO)

2) A Pillar is a High-Leverage Activity

3) A Pillar is Something You Know How to Do Effectively

4) A Pillar Can Be Measured on a Weekly Basis

5) A Pillar is an Action or Predictable Result

6) A Pillar isn't a Habit

STEP 4: Rank Your Potential Pillars by Impact

Rank your potential pillars by the size of their positive impact on your business using the question:

"If I can complete only one pillar from this list each week, which one would have the biggest positive impact on my business?"

Then ask the question repeatedly until you've ranked all the remaining potential pillars. <u>When you answer this question, ignore the time needed to complete the pillar.</u> After all, a 30-minute pillar may have a bigger impact than a two-hour one.

When you answer this question, also consider the "bleed effect." That is, you should consider how completing the pillar affects other potential pillars and different areas of your business. For example, one of my clients swears that an old pillar still profoundly affects every aspect of his life. We put in place a pillar that he must be in bed before 11 p.m. four nights a week. This allowed the former night owl to wake up much earlier, which led to hours of uninterrupted production prior to his first meeting. This single pillar had a domino effect by giving him the time to work on other pillars and PRO activities.

In the world of health, a pillar with the potential for a large bleed effect is "Create a Shopping List." If every week, before shopping, you created a list of healthy snacks and ingredients to make quick, healthy meals, the effect would impact everything else. You would be more likely to come home with the right items. You would be more likely to snack healthy. You would be more likely to prepare meals ahead of time, which can also be a pillar. You would be less likely to order out because you would have what you needed to make healthy meals quickly. The pillar of creating a shopping list has a bleed effect on everything else.

In their book, *The One Thing*, Gary Keller and Jay Papasan ask an excellent question for identifying potential bleed pillars:

"What's the one thing I can do, such that by doing it, everything else will be easier or unnecessary?"

I remember the first time I read this question. I instantly thought, "This is a great question for identifying super pillars!"

STEP 5: Select Your Pillars

The most common question I'm asked regarding pillars is: "How many should I have?" Every business, project, and person is different, so prescribing an exact number isn't realistic. Using the method below, most of my clients and partners wind up with between three and six, though some have less, and some have more.

The rule to trim down your list of potential pillars, now ranked in order of impact, is simple. Working from top to bottom, cut off the list at the point where you can complete your pillars during even your busiest <u>full</u> week. Later in the book, you'll learn how to modify pillars for shorter weeks.

Now you have your first set of pillars to execute on. However, as I discuss in the chapter 4, you'll likely revise this list.

Chapter 2: Critical Points

- A pillar is an activity, <u>meeting specific criteria</u> that when executed on consistently, has a <u>disproportionately</u> positive impact on the health and/or growth of your business.

- Correctly identifying your pillars requires some trial and error.

- You can generate potential pillars by asking a series of specific questions about bottlenecks in your business, skills you need to learn, and strategic activities that can make your actions more impactful.

- To be considered for selection, potential pillars must meet the following six criteria.

  - A Pillar is an Activity in the Proactive/Significant Category (PRO)

  - A Pillar is a High-Leverage Activity

  - A Pillar is Something You Know How to Do Effectively

  - A Pillar Can Be Measured on a Weekly Basis

  - A Pillar is an Action or Predictable Result

  - A Pillar isn't a Habit

- Final selection is based on ranking potential pillars according to their impact and leverage, then cutting off the list based on what you can realistically accomplish in a busy week.

CHAPTER 3

CASE STUDIES

Joanne - Outside Sales Professional

Joanne is an outside sales professional with whom I've been working for almost two years. When we met, she was burned out on her job and unhappy with her health. She was a hard worker who'd built a good client base. But she felt she'd plateaued and was just going through the motions. She wanted to get better.

Based on her goals and the bottlenecks in her business, we identified the following pillars:

Schedule 7/15
Send 5 NSTs
2 Hours STA
3 Workouts

Schedule 7/15 – This means that Joanne will schedule 15 meetings per week. This pillar ensures that Joanne will consistently be in front of clients. Scheduling future meetings was something Joanne often did in spurts and on which she procrastinated.

You probably noticed that the pillar doesn't say she'll "have" 15 meetings per week. She can't control whether she has 15 meetings in a given week. That's determined by past scheduling and current circumstances, such as cancellations and holidays. However, Joanne can control whether she schedules 15 future meetings. Having 15 meetings is a goal. Scheduling 15 meetings is a pillar.

Joanne's scheduling pillar can be categorized as a "predictable result." Although this pillar requires another party to schedule a meeting, Joanne's history demonstrates that if she makes enough calls and sends enough emails, she can realistically schedule 15 meetings.

The number seven, a criterion, means that seven or more of Joanne's scheduled meetings will be with clients who meet a predetermined standard of previous sales production.

Send Five NSTs – Each week, Joanne sends five of her clients a Non-Sales Touch (NST) to strengthen relationships and stay top of mind. NSTs are personalized communications or gifts unrelated to Joanne's products or services. Although sending NSTs is a well-known practice in business to business sales, creating a pillar around NSTs gives Joanne the weekly consistency that leads to better results.

Two Hours STA – Joanne's third pillar is to spend two hours per week improving her skill set, or sharpening the ax (STA) – specifically, reading books or listening to training on business and personal development. Sharpening the ax is a high-leverage activity for Joanne because, in addition to improving her business, she can help clients improve their own businesses. In an industry with many commoditized products, this gives her a significant edge.

Three Workouts – Earlier, we discussed that exercise is a PRO category activity. It has a positive effect on your health over time, but neglecting it doesn't have immediate consequences. Joanne determined early on that if she was going to develop the habit of executing on her pillars every week, she wanted them to bleed into her personal life.

The pillars above represent Joanne's original pillars, but pillars change over time. Since we identified her original pillars, she's increased her weekly NSTs to 10 and her workouts to four. Joanne also eliminated the

STA pillar because she now enjoys and habitually reads books and listens to training. Finally, she added a pillar of reaching out to five people a week who have a potential sale in the pipeline. This pillar we termed "pipeline touches" is a direct result of the increased activity levels her original pillars created.

Joanne started executing on her original pillars in the third quarter of 2015. In 2016, her sales increased by 70 million dollars, which equaled 40% year over year growth. During the same time frame, she lost 36 pounds. By identifying and executing on the right pillars, many people have learned what Joanne did: Improvements in one area of your life can fuel an upward spiral in many areas.

Note: Earlier in the book, I stated that the Pillar System helps you work on your business instead of just in your business. This case study is a perfect example. While most outside sales professionals are always trying to have "more" meetings, a ceiling exists in terms of the number of quality meetings one can have in a week. The only way to grow past this ceiling is to make more money per meeting. Joanne's professional pillars do this. The scheduling pillar ensures she's in front of clients who are more likely to buy. The NST pillar helps her make sales outside of meetings. The STA pillar makes her meetings more effective. The pipeline touch pillar increases her chances of getting a sale from a previous meeting. These all increase her "per-meeting" sales number.

Wayne - Outside Sales Professional

I chose Wayne as the second case study because he holds the same position in the same company as Joanne. This allows me to highlight something I said earlier. Identifying pillars isn't about finding "the" key; it's about finding "your" key. Pillars will vary from person to person depending on the bottlenecks they face and the activities likely to create the biggest positive impact.

Wayne's current pillars are as follows:

Schedule 12/15
Send 5 NSTs
1 Content
Update Pipeline Spreadsheet
30 Minutes Cleaning Office

Schedule 12/15 — As part of his weekly scheduling plan, Wayne must schedule 15 future meetings, of which at least 12 are Million Dollar Meetings (MDMs). MDMs are meetings with clients who did at least one million dollars in business last year or who are on pace for one million dollars in the current year. In recent years, Wayne has been slowly increasing the number of MDMs he must schedule to hit his pillar. Wayne's overall meetings haven't increased, but he's meeting with people who are more likely to purchase. This is a great example of tightening the criteria around your pillars to grow your business; a concept discussed in the next chapter.

Send Five NSTs — Five weekly Non-Sales Touches are similar to Joanne's.

One Content — Wayne's commitment to effective messaging has been a key to his success. This includes creating effective prospecting emails, developing effective talks, and creating stories about his products that make them easy to buy. Each week, Wayne commits to creating one piece of content (e.g., a prospecting email) or spending one hour working on his messaging (e.g., refining a talk). Since Wayne isn't answering emails or meeting with clients, many of his colleagues fail to see content creation as work. And even those who see the value in working on their messaging tend to abandon it during busy weeks. Wayne's pillar is designed to ensure this doesn't happen.

Update Pipeline Spreadsheet – Each week, Wayne opens the spreadsheet containing sales opportunities in the pipeline and updates it based on the previous week's meeting notes. He then reviews older entries to identify opportunities about which he should contact clients. This pillar is a simple pass or fail. Depending on the week, Wayne can complete this pillar in 10 to 45 minutes. This isn't much time, but consistently staying on top of potential opportunities has a huge impact on his business.

This pillar illustrates what I discuss in the next chapter about using pillars as organizational tools. Many salespeople keep notes on meetings and potential opportunities. However, few of them consistently access this information once it's been entered. Wayne's pillar to "Update Pipeline Sheet" directs him to do this every week.

30 Minutes Cleaning Office – Wayne has a pillar to clean and organize his office for 30 minutes every week. He found that the clutter in his office adversely affects his ability to work with a laser-like focus on the task at hand. A simple 30-minute "cleanse" creates an environment that maximizes productivity throughout the week. A seemingly mundane task turns out to be a very high-leverage activity!

Since establishing his first set of pillars almost five years ago, Wayne has more than tripled what was already a significant income and recently wrapped up his best year ever.

Jack - Financial Advisor

Note: Financial advisors are a good group for case studies because they're both sales professionals and entrepreneurs running their own businesses. I again provide two case studies for comparison.

By Jack's own standards, he was finishing up a tough year when he started working with someone whom I'd trained on the Pillar System. After speaking with Jack, my client determined that the bottleneck in Jack's business wasn't a lack of knowledge, skills, or work ethic. Instead, he simply wasn't spending enough time in front of prospects and existing clients.

Together they established the following pillars:

30 Minutes Strategy Session
Schedule 8 Prospect or Client Appointments

30-Minute Strategy Session – Jack's 30-minute strategy session, a strategic pillar, was created with the goal of slowing him down long enough to prioritize his activities for the coming week. On the surface, 30 minutes doesn't seem like a long time. However, when you're alone with your thoughts and a blank piece of paper, it's plenty of time to prioritize your week. For many professionals, it's 30 minutes more than they currently spend. And it's 30 minutes that can save them many hours of wasted time during the week.

Schedule Eight Client or Prospect Appointments – Jack's strength was his ability to gain trust and bring in more assets when meeting with current and potential clients. To capitalize on this strength, he created a scheduling pillar to ensure he was consistently in front of clients and prospects. Each week, Jack works off a prioritized list, created during his strategy session, to schedule at least eight future appointments.

At first glance, Jack's pillars almost seem too simple to significantly change his business. However, about a year after Jack started using the Pillar System, I had a chance to meet him at a workshop I conducted. He told me he'd more than doubled his new client totals and tripled his new assets as compared to the previous 12 months!

Max - Financial Advisor

Max is an established financial advisor who built his business through networking events and prospecting business owners. Today Max spends most of his time in the office "managing" his clients and business. The consequence has been a reduction in the new client acquisition he needs to balance client attrition.

Max and I established the following pillars:

Schedule 1 Social/Networking Event
Schedule 2 Phone Interviews
Send 3 NSTs
1 hr Referral Training

Schedule One Social/Networking Event – After analyzing Max's client list, we found that a large percentage of his revenue came directly and indirectly from past social and networking events. Although on the surface, spending time out of the office seemed counterproductive, the numbers showed that there was no better use of his time. By scheduling one future event per week, we could guarantee that Max would attend an average of one event per week. We also decided he'll increase this number to two events after he hires a junior advisor.

Schedule Two Phone Interviews – Max is concerned that he can't properly service existing clients if he spends too much time at networking and social events. To address this concern and increase his capacity for new clients, Max decided to hire a junior advisor. To ensure that Max consistently looks through incoming resumes, we put in place the pillar of scheduling two future phone interviews each week. Stand-out candidates are invited for in-person interviews.

At first glance, it seems Max will be spending too much time reviewing resumes and interviewing candidates. But what could be a better use of his time? Finding the right junior will break open a bottleneck in his business and save him countless hours in the future. If he's "too busy" to do this now, he'll stay "too busy" long into the future.

Send Three NSTs – A large portion of Max's yearly revenue comes from the residual fee he collects for managing his clients' money. This makes client retention as important as client acquisition. The three non-sales touches, like those described above, are designed to strengthen existing relationships. Additionally, they increase chances for referrals. An NST can be as simple as contacting a client who likes fishing about an upcoming boat show and offering to get them tickets. Regardless of whether the client accepts the tickets, the relationship has been strengthened.

One Hour of Referral Training – Like many service professionals, Max would benefit significantly from more consistent referrals. His problem is that he never found an effective way to ask for or orchestrate them. Consequently, asking for a referral once or twice a week doesn't meet the criteria of a pillar because Max doesn't know how to do it effectively.

Instead, we created a learning pillar to spend at least one hour a week learning different referral strategies, ideas, and scripts. A Google search revealed no shortage of information or resources about the topic. It was just a matter of prioritizing weekly learning. I explained that three months from now Max would have about 15 hours of concentrated research and learning. This was likely enough time to find an effective strategy he could begin to execute on.

Brian - Entrepreneur

The blessing of being an entrepreneur is that you're free to pursue what you want, in the way you want. However, if you're not strategic and disciplined, this blessing becomes a curse. It's easy to jump from business to business under the delusion that one is a "serial" entrepreneur. It's also easy to jump from strategy to strategy and idea to idea within an existing business. Over time, either your finances implode, or you learn that to be successful, you need more strategy and focus than you ever did as an employee. The Pillar System is designed to give entrepreneurs the strategy and focus they need to succeed.

For this book, I decided there's no better case study than myself, so let me catch you up. I'm writing this section at the beginning of 2017. Having wrapped up my last two ventures in 2013, I've spent the past few years helping other professionals and companies through consulting and training while looking for my next venture.

My pillars as of the time of this writing are:

```
Excel 100
1 Content
5 Pillar Plan
3 Workouts
```

Excel 100 – To ensure a steady flow of fresh leads for my consulting and training business, I reach out to 100 potential customers weekly. I reach out through email, phone, and physical mailings. I count both the initial attempt and the follow-up attempts for those who show interest. Depending on the type of prospect and where we are in the sales cycle, the goal of these connections is to drive them to sign up for an email list or to get a phone appointment.

The Excel part of the pillar relates to the discussion in the next chapter about reference documents. I'm constantly thinking about marketing messages and learning about new ways to connect with prospects. I jot these ideas down on my weekly index card (discussed in Chapter 4); the ones that survive the week are put into an Excel spreadsheet. This pillar prompts me to look at that Excel sheet and then take the time to determine the 100 best prospecting and follow up targets, along with the contact method and message.

One Content – The Excel 100 pillar is designed to bring leads in the door. The One Content pillar is designed to nurture those leads and increase the chances they join my list, agree to a phone call, or become clients. It ensures that I create at least one piece of valuable content or spend one hour on a larger piece of content, for this specific purpose. Examples of content include reports, audio training, and emails designed to educate prospects and motivate them to engage with me.

Five Pillar Plan – This pillar ensures that I spend at least five hours a week on my pillar plan. The pillar plan involves the writing of this book and creating the accompanying online and offline resources to support and market it.

Three Workouts – Like Joanne, I've combined my personal pillars with my professional pillars. I don't separate them because I believe that my overall health and confidence directly affect my business and vice versa.

CHAPTER 4

WORKING WITH YOUR PILLARS

Reviewing, Refining, and Changing Pillars

Pillars are changed for two reasons. Either they aren't the right ones to achieve your current set of goals, or your goals or circumstances change. To determine whether you currently have the right pillars, ask the following question at the end of a week during which you executed on your pillars:

"Regardless of my current week's results, do I know beyond a shadow of a doubt that if I keep executing on my pillars, my business is moving in the right direction and it's just a matter of time and pressure until I hit my goal?"

If the answer is "no," you don't have the Friday night feeling and you don't have the right pillars. However, take your time to answer the question. It isn't easy to project out into the future. Remember, pillars work on the compound effect. You must continually execute on your pillars week in and week out to see results. For this reason, you can't expect to see game-changing results after you hit your pillars for a few weeks. However, you should see small wins and feel like you're on the right track.

You should also change pillars when your business goals or circumstances change. This often happens at the beginning of new ventures or when you have a seasonal or cyclical business. I'm currently working on the book you're reading and the online resources to support it. As you can imagine, there are many different steps involved in this, and what I focus on changes with each step. Consequently, the pillar I've put in place is based on hours, not a specific activity. Using a timer, I work on the book and online resources for at least five hours a week. Once the book and online resources are completed, my focus will be on marketing. I can see myself replacing the five-hour-a-week pillar with specific marketing pillars (e.g., scheduling two telephone interviews a week, creating one piece of marketing content each week).

Reviewing, refining, and changing pillars is normal, especially at the beginning. Reviewing your pillars forces you to constantly ask yourself about the best use of your time. That alone makes them a powerful tool in your business.

The downside to having the option of changing and adjusting pillars is you may replace ones you don't like doing with easier ones that have less impact. However, the six characteristics are a built-in check against this. In addition, it won't be long until you don't have the Friday night feeling.

Incorporating Pillars into Your Work Week

One of the highlighted benefits of the Pillar System is an increase in your day-to-day and hour-to-hour clarity. To receive this benefit, you must understand how to incorporate pillars into your work week.

Your first priority is to tackle your Urgent/Significant (US) tasks. These are usually a combination of scheduled activities coupled with incoming requests that you must handle to avoid immediate and significant consequences. This doesn't mean you need to schedule US tasks at the beginning of the day. It just means you don't work on your pillars when you have a scheduled or time-sensitive US task. In fact, when possible, it's better to schedule US activities later in the day. Chapter 5 discusses this in more detail.

Your second priority is to execute on your pillars until they're done. After you've completed your pillars for the week, or when you're done working on them for the day, you can focus on completing insignificant tasks. For maximum efficiency, you should complete insignificant tasks in concentrated bursts as described in the next section. Because insignificant tasks aren't a priority, some of them will fall through the cracks. That's ok — you can't do it all. If too many don't get done, leading to a major issue, you have too much on your plate. You need to either say no to more tasks or get assistance with them. However, don't replace pillars with these insignificant tasks; otherwise, you might quickly fall into the trap of being busy instead of productive.

Finally, be aware of two additional activity types you may need to incorporate into certain weeks. The first type is the long-term US activity. These are projects or deliverables that have a future deadline, but require you to start working on them now if they're to be completed on time. Examples might include prepping materials for a future meeting, finishing a landing page for an ad campaign set to run, or creating slides for a scheduled webinar.

The second type is the non-pillar PRO activity. These may include refining a website page to increase conversions or creating a short-term email campaign you want to test. Sure, you can keep pushing them into the future, but there's a large and positive benefit to completing them. In the case of these two activity types, you must decide where they fit on the priority spectrum – after pillars, but before you complete every insignificant task on your list.

Rocks in a Bucket

Another way to look at incorporating pillars into your week is to adapt the "filling a bucket with rocks" analogy made popular by Dr. Stephen Covey. In the pillar version, think of the space in an empty bucket as the time you spend working each week. The first rocks you put in the bucket are the big rocks – in our example, your US activities. In any business, the US activities determine the room left for other tasks. If this doesn't make sense, please reread the section on US activities.

The medium rocks – your pillars – go in next. In other words, when you're not directly involved in US activities, your pillars are your priority. Finally, after you complete your pillars or finish working on them for the day, you can fill the remaining space with sand (insignificant activities). When you run your week this way, you'll notice the sand eventually overflows. This means you're omitting the right things. Most of us understand at a logical level that we'll never get it all done. The real breakthrough is when we become ok with this fact.

How you should operate   *How most people operate*

Typically, people operate by putting in the large rocks first, then pouring in the sand. The result is that you intentionally or unintentionally run out of the time and energy you need to execute on your pillars. Sure, there's no immediate consequence, and you kept busy all week, but the pillars that drive the long-term health and growth of your business are left out. It's the consistent execution of your pillars that drives the <u>quantity</u> and <u>quality</u> of your future US activities. For example, if you're in sales, a prospecting pillar will drive the amount of future sales presentations (US activity). And a pillar to create a hit list prior to prospecting will increase the quality of the prospect in those meetings.

Playing in the Sand – Handling Insignificant Activities

As discussed earlier, insignificant activities range from trivial non-work distractions to low-priority tasks that require completion at some point. The goal of the Pillar System isn't to ignore the insignificant activities that require your attention, but rather to put them in their proper context.

Although insignificant activities are last on the priority list, there are situations when you can work on them before completing your weekly pillars. If you have 15 minutes between calls, you may find this time better suited to working on insignificant activities instead of working on a pillar.

If toward the end of a day you run out of the mental energy you need to execute on your pillars, spending time on insignificant tasks is justified.

There are two keys to efficiently executing on your insignificant activities. The first key is to prioritize at a macro level. Don't get bogged down in a complicated ranking system to prioritize your insignificant tasks. Instead, take a few minutes before you start and highlight or write down a group of the most important ones.

The second key is to work on them with concentrated bursts of effort I refer to as "flash hours." Set a timer, eliminate distractions, and knock out one task at a time in order of priority. So many of us underestimate what we can do in 30 to 60 minutes of uninterrupted time.

Flash hours are times to focus. They don't represent free time, nor are they times to multi-task. Multi-tasking to increase productivity is a myth I discuss in chapter 5. Although you may believe you'll get more done, you'll actually get much less done.

When you use flash hours, pay close attention to repetitive tasks. If any patterns emerge, seriously consider delegating the task. Delegation is a tool that many entrepreneurs and professionals use poorly or not at all. If you're in this camp, here's an exercise to wake you up. Determine your hourly rate by dividing your yearly income or goal by 2,000. If it exceeds $30 per hour, you're probably losing money by not outsourcing or delegating repetitive, easy-to-do tasks.

Modifying Pillars for Shorter Weeks

The pillars you select are based on your busiest full week. However, due to travel, sickness, holidays, short-term projects, and a myriad of other reasons, you often don't have a full week in which to operate. During shortened weeks, modify your pillars to a realistically achievable level. This prevents you from "breaking the chain" and helps make pillar execution a habit. To effectively modify your pillars, consider two things.

First, modify your pillars <u>before</u> you start the week, before you type your first email or tackle your first task. By first modifying your pillars and then executing them, you continue the valuable mental pattern of executing a pre-determined plan. The inferior but common alternative is to reflect on the week and justify your reduced results. "I did well considering it was a short week." This sends the wrong message to your brain. Don't lie to yourself. Instead, modify your pillars in advance and execute on them.

The second thing to consider is how you modify your pillars. You should reduce your pillars based on 80/20 thinking. Just like everything else, some pillars have a bigger impact on your business than others. Eliminate or reduce activity levels on those pillars with the least impact until you have a realistic list you can complete during the modified week.

A mistake, or excuse, you want to avoid is modifying your pillars during short weeks you could still complete them. For example, if you're traveling on a Thursday and Friday but you normally complete most of your pillars on your Monday and Tuesday office days, you may not need to modify your pillars.

Pillars as Organizational Tools

Reference Documents

When correctly set up, pillars are an effective tool for organizing your work. I run all my ventures from an index card and a legal pad. The index card is my weekly strategy. The legal pad is my daily plan of action and my calendar for the day. I'm able to work with such a simple system because of reference documents.

Reference documents are electronic or physical files, documents, or folders that pillars direct you to use. For example, if one of your pillars is to create two pieces of social media content a week, you can store ideas for content on an Excel spreadsheet or Word document. Unlike most idea lists, you won't forget it exists because your pillar requires you to access it for completion.

I once developed a personal pillar for a client to "read family index card." He wanted to do more with and for his family, but the years seemed to keep flying by. He'd usually create a list of things around the New Year, but it wasn't long before he forgot about it. With that in mind, he created a card (reference document) containing a list of the things he wanted to do throughout the year. Because he was committed to pillar execution, he always pulled out that card to complete his pillars. Some weeks he put the card right back, but other times he took action or put action steps on his daily list. Talk about big results for little effort. I was in his office a few months later and I saw the card by his desk with check marks all over it!

Weekly Planning

A weekly plan for those using the Pillar System will revolve around the tracking of pillar completion. This can be as simple as writing them on an index card, tracking them with check marks and crossing them off when you complete them. Alternatively, you could track them on your laptop or phone. For some, pillars are part of a larger weekly planning and monitoring system; others track only pillars. The most important thing is that your weekly planning system works for you. To help you create one, I've shared a fictional example of my weekly planning system in this section.

At the top left of my weekly index card are fictional directional goals. In this example, they're goals for a monthly revenue minimum and desired body weight. Underneath the directional goals are my current pillars that, when I execute on them weekly, will result in these directional goals being hit. Lower in the left column are US or non-pillar PRO activities, requiring significant time, that I want to work on or complete by the end of the week.

100K Monthly Rev / 175lbs	Ideas	To Do
Pillar 1	Change Email Sig to Include Link?	Book Conf Hotel Dec 1st — *Yellow Highlight*
Pillar 2	Hire PT to Create Land Pages	Fix Quickbooks Bug
Pillar 3	Write Ebook to Give Prospects	Change address with DMV
Pillar 4		Backup Emails
		Update Website - see notes — *Reference doc*
Finish Talk Slides - Tues 3pm — *Yellow Highlight*		
Make Next Week Schedule — *Orange highlight*		
Create New Ad		
	CONT ON BACK	

US (bracket pointing to "Finish Talk Slides" and "Make Next Week Schedule" rows)
Non-Pillar PRO — Create New Ad

Note: I use a large 8x5 index card.

The right column of the weekly index card shows my to-do list. This list contains lower priority professional and personal tasks from all three activity categories. Depending on time, I may or may not complete them during the week.

The middle column of the weekly index card is my place for ideas. Here, I jot down ideas that I come across or that pop into my head. I write them down so they don't distract me, cloud my head, or send me off in a different direction. Quickly taking intruding ideas from "think to ink" has been both liberating and productive for me. When I make the following week's card, I transfer any ideas I still like to their appropriate reference documents. It's amazing how many ideas seem good in the moment, but not the following week.

I keep all the columns short by directing myself to reference documents. For example, "Update Website" refers me to a Word document containing a list of all the changes I want to make on my website. In the rare case that I do run out of room, I simply use the back of the card.

A simple color coding scheme for the card also keeps me organized. If an activity in either column, like "Finish Talk Slides," has a specific deadline, I highlight it in yellow. If I need to finish an activity, like "Make Next Week Schedule," by the end of the week, I highlight it in orange.

Daily Planning

Your whole life you've heard that eating vegetables is good for you. You've heard it so many times, it's probably just background noise. However, this doesn't mean it's not true! The same goes for planning your day. Maybe you've heard you shouldn't start your day until you've finished it on paper. Or you've heard some version of "you must plan your work and work your plan." Yet, like the advice on eating vegetables, this doesn't mean it's not true. I humbly admit that for most of my career I didn't heed this advice. However, a few years ago, when I started consistently planning my days, I couldn't ignore its positive impact on my professional life. So again, I present a fictional example of my daily planning to help you create your own.

I organize my day on a legal pad based on the weekly index card, my calendar, and whatever I didn't finish the day before. In the left margin, I list scheduled calls and appointments along with their times. I highlight them in yellow to indicate they're to be done at a specific time. I divide the remaining part of the legal pad into three columns. In the left column, I write my top two to four priorities for the day. Depending on the day, they may or may not be pillars. I rank them in order of importance by mentally fast forwarding to the end of the day and asking, "If I completed only one task today, which one would I want it to be?" I answer the question based on the consequences of completing or not completing the task. I answer it without considering the time needed or which tasks I'd prefer to work on. Then I ask the question again to determine the second-ranked task and so on.

Everything in Margin Highlighted Yellow			
9am - Rob J	1) Pillar 2	Upload New Training to Site	Mail 1/4 Taxes
9:30 - Lou P	2) Create New Ad	Follow up Craig	Call Vet to Refill
		Send Start Packs to New Sign Ups	
		Calc Pay and Send Julia Check	
12pm - Sales Mtg		Confirm Amy Mtg — *Orange Highlight*	
3pm - Dentist			
7pm - Amy			

A sample of my daily plan on a legal pad

The middle column lists my "to-do" items, including calls to make, things to check on, and small tasks to complete. I work on these miscellaneous tasks in between and after the priority and scheduled tasks of the left column and margin. When possible, I attack them in concentrated bursts and flash hours, as discussed earlier. If my daily activities create additional "to-do" items, I simply expand the list throughout the day. The right column is my personal to-do list that I attack after working hours or on breaks.

Like the weekly index card, I color code items on my daily pad. Orange means the task must be done by the end of the day. Yellow means the task must be done at or by a certain time.

Growing a Business with Pillars

Over time, you can leverage your weekly pillars to grow your business. You can do this in three ways: by increasing the activity levels of individual pillars, tightening the criteria associated with them, or delegating or automating them.

1)   Increasing the Activity Levels of Individual Pillars

Increasing the activity levels of individual pillars should be done slowly and incrementally to prevent a backslide in pillar execution. As stated earlier, with regards to developing the habit of pillar execution, it's more important to hit a smaller number than *almost* hit a larger number. Remember, an increase of one repetition a week adds 50 repetitions to your yearly total.

2)   Tightening Pillar Criteria

Tightening the criteria around individual pillars is another way to grow your business. For example, if a realtor has a pillar of connecting with five "For Sale by Owner" listers per week, he can keep the pillar at five, but tighten the criteria to houses with a sales price of over $250K. Even if his conversion ratio stays the same, those he does convert will pay higher commissions.

Here's another example. Let's say your pillar has you connect with two current customers per week to see if they want additional services. You might increase your pillar's effectiveness by adding the criterion that you'll call on only customers with 20 or more employees. This will increase the likelihood of larger, more profitable sales.

3) Delegating or Automating Pillars

If you're reading this book, you likely get paid or rewarded for results instead of hours. Consequently, you should always be looking to leverage employees, partners, technology, and vendors. Delegating or automating the completion of individual pillars is an effective way of doing this. For example, if you're a consultant who's using marketing pillars to grow your clientele, eventually you'll be spending more time working with clients. This leaves you with less time to complete your marketing pillars. To avoid the common feast-or-famine trap, delegate some or all of your marketing pillars so that you can continue generating fresh leads.

If you're looking to build a business that will scale or run when you're not present, you'll eventually need to delegate and/or automate some pillars. You'll also need to put in place systems or people to handle the increased US activities that result from pillar execution (e.g., order fulfillment). The long-term goal is to be in a position where your pillars are strategic (e.g., spending time finding new markets).

Note: Delegate the completion of pillars, not the identification of pillars, unless the person fully understands the concepts in this book.

If you're experiencing anxiety about delegating, you're not alone. The very idea troubles entrepreneurs and professionals. We fear losing control and often assume we can do it better. And without the pillar system or a similar strategy, we may not have the clarity to delegate effectively. If we delegate without clarity, the ensuing confusion can lead us to grab back the duties ourselves to make it "easier." We become the bottleneck in our own business.

One of my clients, who was good at raising venture capital, wanted me to help him with an ad campaign and messaging strategy. However, there was a problem. When he sought funds, he didn't focus on our evolving marketing plan. His lack of marketing pillars, which would have given him clarity and focus, prevented him from delegating to his staff. Consequently, when he was raising funds, everything came to a halt.

This story illustrates the importance of developing the correct pillars for your project or business. By identifying them, you can delegate the right pillars to the right people. When people who work for and with us clearly understand their priorities, they're empowered to execute them with autonomy and they often excel in ways we couldn't.

Chapter 4: Critical Points

- Consistently review your pillars to make sure they're the right ones for your current circumstances and goals.

- Your week is built around your Urgent and Significant (US) activities. Outside of US activities, pillars should be your next priority, followed by insignificant activities. This ensures that the tasks you don't finish are the least important ones.

- Lump together insignificant activities and attack them in concentrated bursts to maximize efficiency.

- You can modify pillars for short or unique weeks. However, modify them before you work on them.

- When you've set them up correctly, pillars serve as great organizational tools for your business or project. Reference documents are electronic or physical documents that pillars direct you to access.

- You can grow your business with pillars by increasing activity levels, tightening up criteria, and/or delegating and automating them.

CHAPTER 5

EXECUTING ON YOUR PILLARS

Clearly, I'm biased with respect to the simplicity and effectiveness of the system this book presents, but I also know that <u>information isn't enough</u>. Think about the treasure trove of information about eating healthy, exercising and saving for retirement…yet most people fall short in these areas. Heck, if information was enough, we'd all have six packs!

The Pillar System is no different. Your pillars aren't worth the index card they're written on unless you execute on them consistently. This chapter lays out the plan for turning pillar execution into a habit.

Find a Qualified PG Partner

"If you want to go fast, go alone. If you want to go far, go together."
— *African Proverb*

When you have a partner familiar with the Pillar System, your ability to identify the right pillars and execute on them significantly increases. I refer to this type of partner as a PG (productivity giant) partner because, as you'll soon see, they're much more than just an accountability partner.

One reason a PG partner is valuable is that we often need to be reminded, not taught. According to this idea, which I learned from Chris Widener, just because we know something is true or effective doesn't mean we always apply it in our day-to-day business. These reminders have led to many breakthroughs for my partners, my clients and me. We even went so far as to invent the word *re-epiphany* to describe them.

In addition to reminding us what we know, a qualified PG partner can offer insights we can't reach on our own. The way we perceive our business is often different from reality. A second set of qualified eyes can provide insights that remove the bias of being too close to your own project, product, or business. Your PG partner doesn't have to be in a similar field. PG partners from other fields can be helpful because they don't share your assumptions. With a fresh perspective, they often yield valuable insights. I've helped people from industries in which I have no experience. Conversely, people outside my own field have helped me.

Although Darren Hardy, former publisher of Success magazine, is talking specifically about hiring a coach, his passage below perfectly describes the advantages of outside help.

The best in the world have the best in the world advising, consulting and coaching them. It's one of the greatest ways they gain an advantage over their competitors.

The best golfer, tennis player, baseball pitcher, singer, even surgeon, CEO and top entrepreneur all invest in highly paid advisors and coaches. Why? This is a massively critical point about high performance.

*There is a phenomenon called **unconscious incompetence**, meaning, you don't even know when you aren't doing something correctly or to the best of your ability. It takes someone outside of you to observe, identify, prod, and counsel you in order to bring awareness to the adjustments needed to take your performance to the next level.*

A top CEO once said to me, "You can never pay too much to rent someone's eyes, mind, and experience."

If you want to take your life to the next level, you too will want to seek out the best advisors and coaches to help get you there.

Criteria for Selecting a Qualified PG Partner

Whether your prospective PG partners are coaches, friends, or business associates, they should meet the following criteria:

1)   They must be working to improve their own businesses and personal skills via books, seminars, podcasts and other means. If they aren't, they likely won't help you.

2)   They must be more than an accountability partner. Your rela-
        tionship must go beyond the simple "Let's check in on Fridays to
        ensure we hit our goals." Without a deeper relationship, this type
        of system rarely works for extended periods. My PG partner and
        I talk five to seven times a week. Some calls take a few minutes,
        others an hour. It's one of the most valuable uses of our time.

3)   They must continually ask you the right questions even if you
        give them the questions in advance. They should hold a mirror
        up to your face and dig for any disparities between what you <u>say</u>
        you need to do and what you <u>actually</u> do.

4)   They shouldn't take anything you say at face value. Instead, they
        should challenge your assumptions. This will prevent you from
        acting on mistaken thoughts and views that you assume are true.

5)   They must understand the importance of reminding you what
        you already know and what's worked in the past. Without a
        doubt, the biggest benefits I've received from my PG partner are
        the re-epiphanies I previously discussed.

6)   They must be reliable and engaged. They should enjoy the pro-
        cess and feel that they're benefiting from the relationship. With-
        out enjoyment and benefit, the relationship will wither.

7)   They should be open to a two-way, mutually beneficial relation-
        ship. When you become a better coach, you become a better stu-
        dent…and vice-versa. Iron sharpens iron. PG partners sharpen
        PG partners.

8)   They must be someone with whom you feel comfortable sharing
        your personal and business finances if necessary. If you feel the
        need to impress a PG partner or hide information from them,
        the relationship won't work.

The Mindset of Pillar Execution

You need to know, with 100 percent confidence that, if you hit your pillars, you'll hit your goals. <u>If you don't have this confidence, you have the wrong pillars</u>. Your pillars must be your focus. Either you execute them weekly or you outsource them, but they must get done. It's a pass or fail system. If you hit them, you'll still have time for other important tasks. The things that fall through the cracks are those that should fall through the cracks. One hundred percent efficiency isn't your goal – results are.

Pillar execution is extremely important, but not necessarily extremely difficult. Many people find that completing their weekly pillars is relatively easy. However, they find not completing them to be even easier.

You must have the mindset of following your plan instead of your feelings. The Pillar System gives you peace of mind that you're doing the right thing no matter how you feel at a specific time. If you don't want to feel guilty or depressed about your progress, hit your pillars week in and week out and watch these feelings diminish.

Process vs. Event Thinking

Ponder this question: "Why doesn't your business improve when you learn new things?" You read books, attend training, and hear about techniques with which others are having success. However, in the end, you see little to no improvement in the desired area.

In a way, this is a trick question. When it comes to learning valuable skills, reading a book or attending a seminar isn't "learning." Rather, it's "learning about." Reading or hearing information is an <u>event</u>. Learning valuable skills is a <u>process</u>.

The key to improvement is to maintain process thinking, not event thinking. People with event thinking attend my training on writing effective sales emails and leave thinking they know how to do it. Shortly afterward, the same people say, "I tried it. It didn't work." But if you try something a few times and stop, sorry, your feedback isn't credible.

If you can learn a new skill quickly, the skill isn't very valuable to the marketplace. McDonalds can quickly train its staff to increase sales by teaching them to ask, "Would you like fries with that?" or "Would you like to make that a meal?" Consequently, the staff is easily replaceable and paid accordingly.

People with process thinking realize that a learning curve exists. They understand that until you dive in, you don't know what you don't know yet. They accept the fact that, to learn valuable skills, they must repeatedly take action, obtain feedback, and adjust accordingly. MJ Demarco's book, *Unscripted*, brilliantly articulates this concept for entrepreneurs.

Like all valuable skills, learning to correctly identify and consistently execute on your pillars is a process. It isn't rocket science, but you won't get it perfect the first time around. If you go in understanding this, you can quickly get through the learning curve and master a strategy that can change your professional life.

"The problem with penning execution is no one knows what execution IS until you're deep in the trenches. And once you're there, the real game begins."
— *MJ Demarco*

Understanding the Compound Effect

Have you ever participated in a diet or exercise program without getting results? For most people, the answer is yes. Now let's rephrase the question. Have you ever participated <u>for a year straight</u> in a diet or exercise program that didn't produce results? Does that change your answer?

The two diet questions above illustrate the compound effect. This is the principle that small changes made over a long period of time yield far better results than attempts to make large changes in a short period of time. Often, the compound effect produces exponential results. This means executing on your pillars in week 30 will yield better results than executing on the same pillars in week 12. This is an open secret to success that few stick around long enough to benefit from.

You must understand the compound effect to develop the long-term mindset you need for the Pillar System. If you don't understand the compound effect, you'll quickly lose belief that weekly pillar execution is worthwhile.

Making Weekly Pillar Execution a Habit

To reap the compound effect's rewards, you must consistently execute on your pillars over a long period of time. You do this by using motivation, willpower and a custom accountability program (CAP) to make weekly pillar execution a habit. However, before I outline the development of your CAP, let's explore motivation, willpower, and habit.

The Limits of Motivation and Willpower

The motivation to act in your best interest is great when you have it. In fact, I discuss strategies below to summon motivation as often as you can. However, even with the best strategies, motivation is unpredictable, unreliable and often fleeting.

Acting on something without motivation requires willpower. The less motivated you are, the more willpower you need, and vice-versa. Unfortunately, willpower is a finite resource. While evidence exists that one can strengthen willpower, for our purposes, basing long-term pillar execution solely on motivation and willpower is a recipe for failure. Instead, the key is to use short-term motivation and willpower, combined with the CAP strategies I discuss below, to develop a habit that will help you in the long term.

"People often say that motivation doesn't last. Well, neither does bathing — that's why we recommend it daily." — Zig Ziglar

Understanding Habit

At its simplest level, a habit is your brain's way of preserving energy by moving repetitive tasks, behaviors and thought processes from the high-energy-consuming part of your brain to the low-energy-consuming automatic brain. This energy-saving system is why we spend most of our day on autopilot.

Think back to when you learned to drive. Your conscious brain was very involved in every turn of the wheel, highway merge, and busy intersection. This is a good thing, as you were driving a two-ton piece of metal at high speed. However, now that you drive day in and day out, to conserve energy, most of your driving has moved to the automated area of the brain. You can now probably drive somewhere and not even remember the trip!

The number-one mistake people make when trying to develop a habit is believing the upfront energy and effort they need to create the habit is the same energy and effort they need to sustain the habit. This causes most people to throw in the towel, not because they can't complete the task that day, but because they don't see themselves doing it for the long term. They've never experienced completing the task with little energy or resistance. This phenomenon is analogous to a spacecraft that uses most of its fuel to break the earth's gravitational pull. However, once it's in outer space, the spacecraft requires very little fuel to operate and stay in orbit.

Developing a habit is like blazing a trail through a jungle. Grab a machete and a jug of water and start swinging. It'll take hard work and many trips, but each trip gets easier than the last as you cut away and stamp down the vegetation. Eventually, you can travel the <u>same trail</u> with minimal effort, long after you've forgotten the hard work you put into creating the trail.

The Unfair Advantage of Turning Pillar Execution into a Habit

The following sentence is the key to long-term success in almost every area of life. I recommend that you read it a few times. <u>If you can repeat</u>

a high-leverage, highly impactful activity long enough to make it a habit, the positive impact will be exponential instead of incremental.

Look around at the people who've been successful for long periods of time or in multiple ventures. Do they appear to be struggling? It almost makes you mad to see how easy they seem to have it. However, if you reverse engineer their success, you'd see that they developed high-leverage success habits over time and are now enjoying the disproportionate benefits an average person will never attain. What's difficult for you is easy for them – so easy, it's probably harder not to do it.

"Success is actually a short race — a sprint fueled by discipline just long enough for habit to kick in and take over." — Gary Keller and Jay Papasan

---

If you've ever gone to the gym early in the morning, you understand this well. You see the same people there every day, and those happy folks have been going for years. When they wake up, their feet take them through the process of going to the gym as automatically as our feet take us to the coffee maker. Most of us understand that the morning gym crew has an advantage over us in the fitness department, but few understand just how big their advantage is. If you had to rank fitness levels by category, you might come up with a system like this:

1) People who exercise consistently

2) People who exercise occasionally (starting and stopping)

3) People who never exercise

In a world where most people have linear thinking, the common perception is that an equidistant difference exists between the categories. That is, people in category two are a step above those in category three, and those in category one are a step above those in category two. However, if we grabbed a group of 40-year-olds and posted pictures of those in categories one and two at the beach, you'd see a major difference. The people in category one would be in much better shape. In fact, most people in category two wouldn't look much different from those in category three.

What if we held a one-mile race between someone in category one, who runs on the treadmill each day, and someone in category two? Technically, the latter participant would come in second place. However, assuming they were able to finish, the time difference between the two participants would be significant.

In the world of ice cream, the top flavors based on US sales are vanilla, chocolate, butter pecan and strawberry (idfa.org). However, a closer look at the numbers reveals that top-ranked vanilla accounts for 30 percent of sales, while second-place chocolate is only 10 percent. In an industry with US sales of over five billion dollars, this means vanilla brings in one billion more dollars than chocolate in the US alone!

Why am I talking about exercising and ice cream? Because in an 80/20, non-linear world, the top tier is exponentially better than the next lowest tier. Those who put in the work to create the right habit benefit disproportionally compared to those who count on motivation and willpower alone.

Because developing a new habit isn't easy, you must choose those habits that will be high leverage. If you make the weekly execution of your pillars a habit, the world is your oyster.

To be clear, I'm not referring to the individual pillars becoming habits; rather, I'm referring to the execution of your current pillars as a whole. This is important to understand for two reasons. First, if an individual pillar becomes a habit, by definition, it's no longer a pillar. Second, and most importantly, your pillars will change over time as you review and refine them according to changes in your circumstance and goals.

When hitting your pillars is as much a part of your work week as going to the office, you've arrived. When not hitting your pillars feels like being on the couch all week, you're in a great place. I hope you're convinced about the value of making pillar execution a habit. Now let's get to work developing the Custom Accountability Program that you'll use to accomplish this.

Creating a Custom Accountability Program

When left to its own devices, the brain takes the path of least resistance – our current habits. Our brains love habits. Habits make life easier. They use little energy. They feel as natural and comfortable as our skin. So, how do we continually hit our pillars long enough for weekly pillar execution to become a habit?

The answer is to use every strategy in your arsenal to push and pull yourself up the hill of weekly pillar execution until you get over the hump of habit formation and enjoy the downhill ride. The strategies you choose comprise your Custom Accountability Program (CAP).

"Custom" is the most important word in "Custom Accountability Program." Why? Because habit-formation strategies that work for one person don't necessarily work for someone else. Not surprisingly, the habit formation literature agrees.

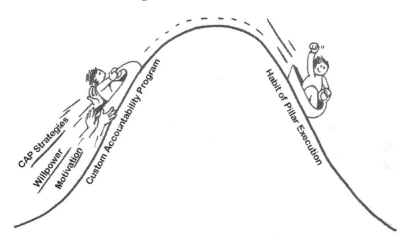

In their book *Change Anything – The New Science of Personal Success*, Kerry Patterson and his co-authors suggest that people become both the scientist and the subject when finding the "changing" strategies that work for them. I use this process when identifying CAP strategies for my clients. We try as many CAP strategies as necessary until we find the lock's combination – a combination they emotionally and intellectually endorse. The reasons are straightforward. To embrace and implement the strategies, my clients must believe in them. If they believe in and implement them, they're more likely to succeed.

To help you develop your CAP, I've listed several strategies below. Use the list as a buffet. Try what you want, use what works and leave the rest. In some cases, you may find a single strategy that gets you over the top. In other cases, you may need to use a few of them. For each strategy you choose, I strongly suggest supplementing the information inside this book with additional in-depth, external resources.

When reading this section, don't assume the strategies with longer sections are superior. Some strategies simply take longer to explain. Similarly, don't assume the strategies appear in order of effectiveness. Also, expect an overlap between strategies. This is intentional. Clarifying and re-presenting concepts somewhat differently make them easier to understand.

If you've found your PG partner, involve him or her in the process. If you haven't found one, work on your own for now, but make it a priority to start looking.

Finally, to select strategies with the best chances of working, consider using Gretchen Rubin's helpful framework to categorize yourself. In her book *Better Than Before*, Rubin identified four categories of people who have different responses to rules and expectations. While everyone has traits from a few of her categories, one category typically dominates. Understanding the categories – and the one category that most describes you – will help you select the most effective strategies. Her categories are as follows:

Upholders – Upholders obey both external and internal rules and expectations. Once they understand the rules and expectations, they don't need much, if any, external accountability. Simply put, they don't want to let down anyone – including themselves. Without rules, they can't operate well. To avoid such situations, they'll often create their own rules.

Questioners – Questioners won't follow rules with which they disagree or believe to be arbitrary. They question all rules and expectations and comply only if they agree with them. They like to prove the way they do something is the right way.

Obligors – Obligors respond to rules and expectations from external sources because they don't want to let down others. They struggle with self-imposed expectations and rules and commonly let themselves down. Often, the result is burnout. The best type of accountability for this group is external accountability.

Rebels – Rebels resist external rules and expectations. Often, they intentionally do the opposite – defy rules and expectations. They have few internal rules. Immediate desires and an "I'll show you" mentality drive them. They rarely have much self-control.

CAP Strategies

Change Your Identity and Standards

This is my favorite strategy for good reason. It's the genesis of my biggest breakthroughs. Psychologically, it makes sense. It stems from the idea that we act like the person we think we are, regardless of how accurate our perception is.

When I transitioned from environmental scientist to entrepreneur, I went out of my way to ensure people didn't think I was a "salesperson." Though I was always selling myself and my product, I tried to convince myself that I wasn't in sales. As I matured as an entrepreneur, I realized this internal contradiction was holding me back. I decided to take ownership of selling. Specifically, I decided to become so good that I could eventually teach others.

It's worth repeating: We act like the person we think we are. This means you can make a <u>conscious decision</u> to become a person who always executes on their pillars. It can be a source of pride that you aren't like the masses who have trouble sticking to any strategy.

A complete identity change in a specific area is easier to implement than a partial one. Ninety-nine percent is much harder than 100 percent. Don't waste energy trying to do this or trying to not do that. Instead, establish a few standards about "who you are" instead of "what you will or won't do." Standards aren't goals or desires; they're your internal boundaries. You'll get much further with a few standards than with a laundry list of things you "want" to change.

A standard acts like a thermostat that returns you to your identity. If you're a clean, healthy eater, having pizza on Friday night won't become a weekend binge. The next morning you'll probably have a healthy breakfast. If your monthly bills average $5,000 and your standard is that you "pay your bills," you'll probably average $5,000 per month in after-tax income. Even when you have high-income months, you'll notice a pattern of moving back to your average. If you start making more money, but your standard doesn't change, you'll notice that your bills tend to increase.

When I help clients become proactive rather than reactive, I usually hear statements like, "I'm not going to answer my phone when I'm working on something important." However, in their voices, I hear the silent escape words "try" and "except when."

The long-term goal isn't to rely on hacks like throwing your phone in the drawer or putting it face down on your desk. Instead, your goal is to "become" a person who ignores the distraction and finishes what you start. When you become this person, you won't need "tricks" to focus on a task long enough to complete it.

Once you decide to change your identity and start consistently hitting your pillars, your small achievements will further cement your identity. This will lead to bigger achievements, and the upward spiral will begin.

Find a Reason to Change

Most of us "want" to progress in our projects and businesses, but our resistance to change and to leaving our comfort zone is often stronger than this desire. If your incentive to change isn't strong and enduring, the simplest of changes will prove difficult.

Your job is to connect with a real and powerful incentive to change, often called your "Why." A real incentive is something that connects with you regardless of how it sounds to others. For example, a client recently told me his incentive to change was the desire to take care of his son. It sounded like the right thing to say, but he has a healthy son, a great family and enough money in the bank to weather many storms. So we dug deeper and found his true incentive, his true "Why." His true incentive likely wouldn't resonate with you, but it does with him, and that's all that matters.

Everyone's incentive is unique. For some people, earning lots of money is the incentive. For others, it's buying this and that. For still others, it's earning and using the money to make life better for people in need. However, money isn't everyone's incentive. An intensely competitive group of people want to show they're the best by crushing the competition. Others simply want to prove someone wrong. For you to excel, you must connect with the critical incentives that motivate you to persist in executing on your pillars.

This section seems so cliché, but if you take the time to find and articulate your Why, your ability to persist will improve. A good place to start is thinking about Daniel Pink's three primary elements of the human drive.

In *Drive: The Surprising Truth About What Motivates Us,* Pink identifies these three elements as:

<u>Autonomy</u> – The desire to create our own direction.

<u>Mastery</u> – The desire to become good at something and the joy of making progress.

<u>Purpose</u> – The desire to do things that matter, and to be a part of something bigger than ourselves.

Remember, your Why doesn't have to sound good or make sense to anybody else. If it gives you the energy you need for the uphill climb to turn pillar execution into a habit, you're on the right path.

Unsubscribe (Saying No)

The unsubscribe strategy works well for those who believe they don't have time to complete their pillars.

As a recovering shiny object junkie, I've subscribed to countless email lists offering ideas for improving my business. The result was an inbox stuffed with good but unconnected ideas that caused me to constantly change course. These changes drained my time and energy.

Eventually, I realized it's better to bring a good idea across the finish line than to continuously seek better ones. Once I internalized this concept, I spent a few hours on a holiday unsubscribing to most of the email lists. The ones I valued most I redirected to a different email address so I could access them proactively if desired. The time and energy saved have changed my business.

Every day you say "no" to things, both intentionally and unintentionally. You can either <u>choose</u> what you say no to or <u>have it chosen for you</u> by saying "yes" to the wrong things. The former is the path to success.

Here is what you must think about.

<u>What</u> must you say no to, so you can execute on your pillars? Specifically, what activities, projects, ideas, and commitments should you remove from your business?

<u>Whom</u> must you say no to, so you can execute on your pillars? This includes, but isn't limited to, customers, colleagues, vendors, employees and personal relationships.

"It's easy to add things to your business, it's terrifying to subtract." — Perry Marshall

---

To unsubscribe successfully, you must establish <u>clear rules</u> about what you say no to. Once you've established these rules, you no longer must "decide" if you should say yes to certain things; the rule decides for you. You'll know you're making progress when you start priding yourself on all the things you say no to – or stop doing as soon as you realize you should have said no.

Time Blocking and Routine

A common belief among those struggling to complete their weekly pillars is that they don't have enough time. On rare occasions, they're correct. In those cases, they simply reduce the number and/or activity levels of their pillars. In most cases, however, the perceived lack of time is a result of spending too much time working on seemingly urgent but less important activities.

If you categorized yourself earlier as an upholder, you'd likely find time blocking to be the easiest solution. Specifically, you'd schedule appointments with yourself to work on your pillars.

If you're not an upholder, and you'll ignore or move these appointments when you're not "in the mood," this type of time blocking won't work. Instead, create a routine by time blocking at the beginning of your day. The more of a routine you create when working on your pillars, the easier you'll find turning pillar execution into a habit. Furthermore, your mental energy will likely be highest at the beginning of the day.

It seems counterintuitive to add appointments when you feel you don't have enough time for your existing commitments. However, it makes more sense when you consider Parkinson's Law – the observation by UK author and historian Cyril Northcote Parkinson that *work expands to fill the time available for its completion.* This means what normally takes eight hours can probably be done in six hours if that's the time you have available. If you budget a few morning hours to work on your pillars, you'll still finish the other "stuff" before the end of the day.

Throughout 2017, I've taken full advantage of Parkinson's law to write a book, execute on my pillars and assist a packed calendar of consulting clients. I've done this by keeping a standing appointment with myself, from 7 a.m. to 10 a.m. every non-travel day, to work on pillars and other PRO activities. This routine gives me plenty of time to speak with clients after 10 a.m.. What it doesn't give me time for is a lot of low-priority tasks and distractions. Want to speak to me at 9 a.m.? Sorry, I'm booked. How does 10 a.m. work? How does next week work? Of course, the occasional exception arises, but it's just that – an exception.

Our misunderstanding of focus is why we underestimate what we can accomplish in an hour, but overestimate what we can accomplish in a week. It's amazing to discover how productive we can be during short, uninterrupted, focused blocks of time. It's sobering to realize how few of these blocks of time we have during the week. That's why it's critical to intentionally schedule and protect them.

Think Big, Start Small

Your initial priority is to develop the habit of pillar execution. By starting small, with fewer pillars and lower levels of activity, you'll initiate several habit-forming principles.

Frequency is the first one. Higher frequency of action augments habit formation. If you start small, you have a better chance of completing your pillars more frequently.

Reducing resistance to action is the second principle. When we complete our pillars more frequently, we strengthen our belief that we can accomplish the task. When our belief is high, our resistance to action is low. When this resistance is low, it's even easier to complete our pillars, thus strengthening our belief. This positive feedback loop begins an upward spiral of pillar execution.

Stephen Guise, author of *Mini Habits: Smaller Habits, Bigger Results*, believes in the power of "stupid, small" habits. His book begins with his experience of doing at least one pushup a day, every day. He could do more than one if he felt like it, but doing just one meant completing the task. After six months, his resistance to exercise decreased and he's now a gym regular.

Starting small is also an effective strategy for overcoming your brain's natural resistance to change. By starting small, you "trick" your brain into changing. You use slight, almost imperceptible changes that don't amount to much individually. However, the compound effect of these small changes is very powerful in terms of developing the habit of pillar execution. This is analogous to the parable of boiling a frog. If you put a frog in boiling water, it will jump out. However, if you put the frog in water and slowly raise the temperature one degree at a time, the cold-blooded frog won't notice and will eventually boil.

Stanford professor B.J. Fogg, one of the premier experts in the science of habit formation, also champions the concept of starting small. His concept of "Tiny Habits" stemmed from his flossing one tooth at a time to form the habit of flossing all his teeth. For an in-depth understanding of how to use Dr. Fogg's strategy, visit his two websites, BehaviorModel. org and TinyHabits.com.

To apply this strategy to pillar execution, start with one or two pillars that require little from you. This will help you string together a series of wins, strengthening your optimism and motivation. For example, your pillars might be scheduling one prospecting meeting a week and working on your sales letter for 15 minutes a week.

Over time, you can increase the activity levels and the number of pillars. The key word is "gradually." If you overload yourself after a series of wins, you'll become discouraged. The result will be a quick loss of the habit-forming momentum you've gained.

Eventually, you want to operate inside what James Clear calls "The Goldilocks Rule." In his whitepaper, *The Scientific Guide on How to Get and Stay*

Motivated, he explains that we experience peak motivation when we operate on the edge of our current ability. It shouldn't be too easy or too hard, but just right.

One Thing at a Time

Intentionally developing a new habit is difficult. Increasing the difficulty, what we think of as one habit is often many habits. For example, if you want to create the habit of exercising in the morning, you'll need to develop multiple habits.

These may include:

- Going to bed earlier

- Waking up earlier

- Putting on workout clothes instead of work clothes

- Going straight to the exercise area or gym instead of to your laptop

    … And you haven't even started working out yet!

A realistic strategy would be to develop the habit of going to bed by a certain time each night. After you're consistently waking up when the alarm rings, you can start getting dressed and heading to your workout room to read for an hour. Once going straight to the workout room is habitual, you can add the workout.

Why did I highlight the difficulty of creating what seemed like one new habit? I want to encourage you to avoid developing new habits or making significant life changes while you're developing the habit of pillar execution. Doing two things at once decreases your odds of succeeding in either area.

"A man who chases two rabbits catches neither." — Chinese Proverb

Change Your Mood

We all procrastinate when we dislike a task or don't "feel" like working on it. Other things look more interesting. They're more inviting. This is an experience we all share. However, once we get into action, it's much easier to remain in action. The key, and often the hardest part, is getting started.

"An object at rest will remain at rest unless acted on by an unbalanced force. An object in motion continues in motion with the same speed and in the same direction unless acted upon by an unbalanced force." — Isaac Newton's First Law of Motion

One strategy to kickstart pillar execution is to intentionally change your mood or emotional state. By giving yourself the initial spark, you can take advantage of the motivation that often comes <u>after</u> you get into action.

The mind-body connection works two ways – from the mind to the body and from the body to the mind. Many people focus on the former and forget the power of the latter. Stub your toe and you'll feel the pain of the body influencing your mind. Walk briskly for 50 minutes on a nice day and your bad mood may disappear. This isn't magic; it's biology. Stubbing your toe and walking briskly both release chemicals that change your emotions. When you change your physiology, you change your "mood."

You can intentionally change your mood in many ways. These include, but are not limited to, exercise, music, watching videos, talking to certain people and changing your environment. For me, talking to certain people and watching certain videos puts me in the mood to attack things. This seems elementary, but it works.

Experiment with things that help you get into a better mental state. When you find them, try to make them easy to do and start. The upfront work involved in putting a link on your desktop, buying exercise bands or loading something onto your playlist will pay big dividends down the road.

Manage Your Mental Energy

As we discussed earlier, your success depends on your ability to focus your limited mental resources on the right activities (i.e., focus management). This section discusses how to increase the availability of these mental resources by allocating them more effectively.

Advances in science have confirmed what most of us experience. Our brains act like muscles, especially when they engage in higher cognitive functions. As with muscles, our brains can fall victim to stress and overuse, which lessen their effectiveness. We even have common terms to describe this phenomenon, such as "burnt out," "hit a wall" and "it hurts to think." Accordingly, you should structure your day with these limitations in mind.

Work on PRO activities at the beginning of the day, when mental resources tend to be the highest. Also, work on US activities that require significant concentration, such as completing a presentation by a deadline, during the early part of the day. When possible, move US activities like meetings to the second part of your day.

Strive to structure the beginning and end of your days. This technique, known as bookending, allows habits to develop at times when you have the most control over your schedule. Consider the habit of working out before you start your workday, the habit of working on your pillars before the phone starts ringing and the habit of flossing before you go to bed.

Ideally, you should structure your entire day so that you work in concentrated 90-minute bursts followed by periods of rest. The idea that we're more productive working in an alternating work and rest cycle stems from what scientists refer to as our ultradian rhythm. Tony Schwartz's book, *The Way We're Working Isn't Working,* offers keen insights into applying this concept to our lives.

In some businesses and projects, this structure isn't ideal or realistic. Road warriors, for example, spend excessive time in the car going from appointment to appointment. If this describes you, I recommend using Monday as an office day to work on your pillars. Then, when you have downtime before, between and after appointments, you can focus on completing any remaining pillars.

If your business requires that you work on your pillars later in the day, take a LONG break before starting. A break will rejuvenate you and reset your day, allowing you to be more productive when you start working again. For example, I'm more productive in the afternoon with a two-hour break followed by 90 minutes of work than when I force myself to work four straight hours. Why? Mental fatigue fosters mistakes, procrastination and trouble concentrating.

Increase Your Mental Energy

In addition to managing your energy throughout the day, you can use scientifically based strategies that increase overall mental energy. This area is beyond the scope of this book. However, Dr. Edward (Ned) Hallowell's book, *Driven to Distraction at Work,* does an excellent job of introducing the "Sensational Six:" sleep, nutrition, exercise, meditation, stimulation, and connection.

Implementing pillars to improve in these areas will have disproportionately positive benefits. For example, the pillar of working out three times a week improves mental energy, confidence, and sleep. A well-rested, confident professional with energy will excel in many areas of business. Because of this connection between personal well-being and professional success, I recommend combining your personal and professional pillars.

Improve Your Focus

Note: This section considers "focus" to mean directing and sustaining your attention and mental resources to successfully complete a task. Thus, when I use the word "focus," I'm also speaking about concentration.

The torrent of distractions in our complex and always-connected world makes it increasingly difficult to focus. Emails, text messages, social media, phone calls and a 24-7 news cycle all want our attention. Together, these seemingly little distractions become a giant magnet pulling our focus away from productive tasks.

But there's good news. You can improve your focus. Daniel Goleman, author of *Focus: The Hidden Driver of Excellence,* highlights the scientific evidence showing that focus works like a muscle. The more we work on it, the stronger it becomes. He explains that "practicing" focus increases our ability to bring our wandering minds back to the task at hand.

Many professionally developed exercises can strengthen your focus. These exercises typically ask you to focus on a task for a short time and to refocus your mind when it wanders or becomes distracted. Over time, you increase the duration of your focus. If this technique sounds familiar, you may have been introduced to meditation.

Meditation asks you to focus on the present, often using your breathing as the target of your focus. When intruding thoughts arrive, you let them pass through and then you refocus. It's no coincidence that a large percentage of highly successful people, from athletes to entrepreneurs, practice some form of meditation.

You can also strengthen your focus throughout the course of a day. For example, you can listen attentively to people and, when your mind wanders, quickly refocus on what they're saying. In *Deep Work*, Cal Newport offers the daily strategy of "embracing boredom" to improve your focus. He suggests challenging the addiction of always needing input by embracing short periods of time during which you do nothing. For example, wait in a line without playing on your smartphone.

One of the simplest ways to improve focus is to stop multi-tasking. Most studies show that people don't actually multi-task; instead, they quickly switch back and forth between tasks. Yes, you can chew gum and walk at the same time, but you can't effectively use the same part of your brain simultaneously for two cognitively demanding tasks. If you're listening to an important conference call while writing an email, you're either missing parts of the call or taking too long to write a subpar email.

The mounting scientific evidence continues to suggest that multi-tasking is nothing more than a productivity myth. An often-cited study from the University of London suggests that multitasking makes people less productive than if they were smoking pot. At best, this isn't a strong endorsement. So, here's some strong advice: Focus on one thing at a time. Forget multi-tasking.

If-Then

The "If-Then" strategy is popular for good reason. It works with, not against, human nature. Many studies have shown that decision making requires the same mental resources as willpower and other cognitive functions. As these resources diminish, the quality of decision making is lessened. To combat this, establish rules by making some decisions in advance. Consider the habits of many successful people who reduce decision making by wearing the same outfits and eating the same foods most days.

A simple method of establishing rules is using the If-Then strategy. Here are a few examples of "If-Then" rules to help with pillar execution:

- **If** I'm traveling overnight, **then** 100 pushups and 50 crunches in my hotel room will count as a workout.

- **If** I don't finish my prospecting calls during my time block, **then** I'll schedule another future prospecting time block <u>before</u> I start my next task.

- **If** someone asks me to commit to something in person, **then** I'll ask them to email the request, so I have time to decide logically instead of emotionally.

- **If** Monday is a holiday, **then** I'll block Tuesday as my office day to focus on my pillars.

Short-Term Rewards

For some people, rewarding oneself for pillar completion is a simple but effective strategy. The weekly reward, like going to your favorite restaurant, should be small but motivating. The more you look forward to it, the greater its motivational power. Larger rewards, like a vacation for 10 weeks of pillar execution, may work at first. However, when your vacation ends, your motivation to work without another big reward on the horizon may end as well.

Many people, including those who earlier identified themselves as "Obligors," may benefit from sharing or giving their reward to someone else. One example is buying a bunch of small-denomination gift cards to a store your significant other likes. Each week, when you complete your pillars, give them a card. In addition to enjoying their happiness, you get a cheerleader on your team.

Ultimately, it's important that motivation for completing your pillars not depend on extrinsic rewards. Using a reward system for too long may cause you to see pillar execution as a weekly obstacle to overcome. Consequently, only use short-term rewards until you start realizing progress through small wins and the feeling that you're moving in the right direction. This feeling of progress will keep you moving toward creating the habit of pillar execution.

Loss Aversion

In the late 1970's, the principle of loss aversion was introduced by a group of researchers, one who went on to win the Nobel Prize. Basically, it states that our aversion to losing something is much stronger than our desire to gain something of equal value. Think of the short-term rewards discussed above. For most of us, the desire to receive a $20 gift card for completing our pillars isn't nearly as strong as our desire to avoid paying a $20 penalty for falling short. The more you value what you're risking, the more powerful your loss aversion.

I'm not suggesting that you burn money, but I've seen some very creative ways to combine loss aversion with other motivators. How about writing a check to a political group you don't support and giving it to someone with instructions to mail it if you don't hit your pillars!

Keep Score

Track the progress and completion of your weekly pillars in a highly visible place. I use the oversized index card containing my weekly plan. It's not fancy, but it's effective. Readily visible check marks and crossed-off pillars create a feeling of momentum and progress.

For many, the challenge is as motivating as what they receive in return. Falling in love with the process is a mindset that feeds off itself. Remember, you use willpower when you <u>don't</u> want to do something! When you want to do something, like add another week of pillar completion to your streak, you become energized.

It's easy to determine when clients are enjoying the game as much as the work. They tell me crazy stories about what they did to complete their pillars. They have an <u>offensive</u> mindset toward executing on pillars and start using phrases like "crushed my pillars." It's no accident that people who enjoy the sense of accomplishment from pillar execution, as much as the Friday night feeling, tend to succeed with the Pillar System.

Use Triggers

Dr. B.J. Fogg's renowned behavior model states that, for a behavior to occur, three elements must be available: motivation, ability, and a trigger. He recommends using existing habits as a trigger to start another activity you want to turn into a habit. For example, when Dr. Fogg was trying to develop the habit of flossing, he used the existing habit of brushing his teeth as the trigger.

If you have trouble starting on your pillars, you might want to consider using an existing habit as a trigger. If the first thing you do in the morning is fire up your laptop, check your email, and plan your day, you could start attacking your pillars for an hour immediately afterward. In this scenario, as soon as you finish planning your day (trigger), you start working on your pillars.

If you don't have an existing habit that would work well as a trigger, create a trigger with a pre-habit ritual. For this to succeed, you must make the ritual extremely easy to do. It can be as simple as setting a timer for 60 minutes before working on your pillars or clearing your desk.

Reward the Bounce Back

When we're developing the habit of pillar execution, we're often hard on ourselves for not completing our pillars by week's end. This is both stressful and counterproductive. Emotionally and motivationally, it can create a downward spiral that makes execution even more difficult the next week.

If you don't hit your pillars one week, don't throw in the towel. The proper response is to complete your pillars the next week. When you bounce back like this, you're in rare air and should be well-rewarded. Why? Because this is when most people quit. In hockey, the top goalies aren't those who never give up a goal. The top goalies are those who don't fall apart after letting one in.

Within your workdays, reward yourself for having the grit to bounce back. If you get distracted while working on a pillar or important task, take pride in re-engaging. Remember, the practice of refocusing when your mind wanders is the key to strengthening your ability to focus. This is a critical skill for success.

You should also take pride in bouncing back from big distractions, like unexpected family issues or computer problems. Don't fall into the trap of all-or-nothing thinking. Don't categorize days as either good or bad. If you do, you'll let larger distractions affect your whole day rather than just the part they affect. Every day won't be productive from start to finish, and unexpected distractions are part of the formula. However, you can be productive during the part of the day that's available. It's good practice to reward yourself for doing the best with what you're given.

Change Your Language

Changing your language is a simple but powerful way to help with pillar execution. The way we speak to ourselves and others influences everything from our mood to our beliefs. By changing our language, we can lower our resistance to doing things we don't like doing. We may even start enjoying some of these activities.

Like many people, I don't like to exercise, but once I'm on my treadmill, the hard part is over. In the past, when I had to schedule workouts in the middle of the day, I labeled the appointments in my calendar as "Brian Time." I associated this term with positive things, such as disconnecting, clearing my brain, and even watching a good training video or TV show.

Here are some additional examples to consider:

Change "I have to" to "I choose to." (This creates a stronger sense of control.)

Change "Asking for the business" or "Following up" to "Collecting money."

Change "Prospecting" to "Digging for gold."

Although these little changes seem insignificant, it's powerful stuff. Changing your language is a core component of cognitive behavior therapy, one of the world's most successful psychological interventions.

Go Public

The strategy of going public is personality-specific. You may find that sharing your pillars with others incentivizes you to hit them out of fear, motivation, or both. For some people, telling their boss or an individual they look up to is just what they need. Others may want to tell colleagues and peers. And these days you can always be brave and tell your social media "friends."

Because I want to set an example, I've found that telling my clients and partners about my pillars is extremely motivating. I've even used the "going public" strategy with individual pillars. In an earlier business, I turned my cold prospecting calls into training opportunities for others. I set aside a time when someone else could be on the line so that they could hear everything. There was no backing out! I also recorded these calls to share with others. Here, my mindset wasn't fear. It was pride. I took pride in setting an example for those who worked with me. I took pride in showing them I was willing to do what I'd taught them to do. I'm not sure how many cold calling sessions I'd have procrastinated on or eliminated if I hadn't "gone public."

External Accountability

As you've probably gathered, I'm a big believer in mentors, coaches, and PG partners. In addition to offering an external set of objective eyes, these individuals can serve as accountability partners. Some people, like obligers, do better when they know that other people have expectations of them. If you do better when someone else is monitoring your progress, external accountability may be an effective strategy.

You can also pay for accountability. If you hate wasting money, paying a coach to keep you accountable can increase your chances of consistently executing on your pillars. A few years ago, I decided to learn how to play the guitar, a skill that demands practice and repetition. I quickly determined that everything I'd need to learn this skill was available free on YouTube. So why did I pay a guitar instructor to come to my house twice a month? You guessed it – accountability. I didn't want him to see me regress and I didn't want to waste money. Predictably, when the instructor stopped coming, my playing time decreased considerably.

Restructure Your Team

We're influenced by the people with whom we regularly interact. In many ways, these people define what's "normal." People who attribute results primarily to external factors, such as the economy and their circumstances, will be cynical about your attempt to change. Conversely, people who see the value in always improving will encourage you.

Clearly, both types of people are in our lives. The key is to recruit and associate with those who facilitate and support growth while avoiding the cynics and people who think they have little influence on their future.

Change Your Environment

Your physical environment has a bigger influence on your focus and emotions than you may realize. Your ability to control your environment at the macro and micro levels will go a long way toward helping you execute on your pillars.

I don't know much about *feng shui*, but I do know that your work area, including your car if you travel, must be conducive to productivity. If you don't like your work environment, you'll resist working. Consequently, you should spend the necessary time and money to create the workspace you need. This could include decorating and arranging your office in a way that makes it comfortable and inspiring. Or it could be as simple as setting up your desk so that you remain clear of anything except the items necessary for your current task.

For many people, working from a different location for some tasks can be productive. If you feel that you need a different location for certain tasks, make sure that's all you use it for. You want to associate the new location with specific tasks, such as prospecting calls or writing. The goal is to get in, produce, and get out.

At a micro level, you must create a work environment that automatically minimizes distraction. This can include hanging signs to keep others away and keeping potential distractions out of reach. Because we tend to leave things as they are, once you've set up things correctly, you're unlikely to change them back.

At a minimum, turn off email, text, social media, and other notifications on your phone and computer. When possible, turn off any devices you don't need for the task at hand. Heresy, I know! If you must write emails to complete a pillar, turn your email program to "offline" until you're finished and ready to send them. If you have a job or personal situation for which you must be "on call," set your phone to alert you when specific contacts call. You can also give these contacts a separate, rarely used office number to call. Almost every potential distraction has a solution if you take the time upfront to prepare for it.

Chapter 5: Critical Points

- Working with a partner familiar with the Pillar System will exponentially increase your chances of success, but you must find "the right" partner.

- Executing on your pillars must be at the forefront of your mental focus.

- Willpower and motivation don't work long term. To realize the beneficial compounding effect of the Pillar System, you must turn weekly pillar execution into a habit.

- This is done by creating a Custom Accountability Program (CAP) using short-term willpower, motivation, and CAP strategies to execute on your pillars long enough for a habit to form. It takes trial and error to determine the CAP strategies that work for you.

ABOUT THE AUTHOR

Brian Margolis is a former environmental scientist turned entrepreneur and the founder of ProductivityGiant.com. Both his accomplishments and failures span a variety of fields. In addition to his own entrepreneurial ventures, Brian currently assists entrepreneurs and professionals ranging from individual sales reps to Fortune 500 companies.

He can be contacted directly at brian@productivitygiant.com

To Learn How We Can Help You or Your

Company Create and Implement a Strategy

ProductivityGiant.com

To Access the Latest Bonus Materials and Training

IndexCardBusinessPlan.com

REFERENCES AND SUGGESTED READING

80/20 Sales and Marketing – Perry Marshall

Better Than Before – Gretchen Rubin

Change Anything – Kerry Patterson et al.

Drive: The Surprising Truth About What Motivates Us – Daniel Pink

Driven to Distraction at Work – Edward Hallowell, MD

Essentialism: The Disciplined Pursuit of Less – Greg McKeown

Influence: The Psychology of Persuasion – Robert Cialdini

Mini Habits: Smaller Habits, Bigger Results – Stephen Guise

Procrastinate on Purpose – Rory Vaden

The 7 Habits of Highly Effective People – Stephen Covey

The 80/20 Principle: The Secret to Achieving More with Less – Richard Koch

The Compound Effect – Darren Hardy

The E-Myth – Michael Gerber

The E-Myth Revisited – Michael Gerber

The One Thing – Gary Keller and Jay Papasan

The Power of Focus – Jack Canfield, Mark Victor Hansen, Les Hewitt

The Power of Habit – Charles Duhigg

The Procrastination Cure – Jeffery Combs

The Psychology of Self-Motivation (Ted Talk – Tedx Virginia Tech) – Scott Geller

The Scientific Guide on How to Get and Stay Motivated (whitepaper) – James Clear

The Slight Edge – Jeff Olson

The Way We're Working Isn't Working – Tony Schwartz

Tools of Titans – Tim Ferris

Unscripted – MJ Demarco

Your Brain at Work – David Rock

Made in the USA
San Bernardino, CA
30 June 2019